As a working Actor/Director, I find this book extremely valuable, not only for the actor just starting out but also for professionals who want to stay on top of their game. It's a conversational and informative skill set that every actor should read. ~ **Richard Kline, Award Winning Actor/Director in Theatre, Television, & Film**

There are thousands of books out there on acting, perhaps only a few are noteworthy. ACTOR MUSCLE by Beverly Leech is in the select group of go-to books for the working actor. Ms. Leech has combined her keen business acumen and her artistic gifts to support an artist in putting their best foot forward in an increasingly competitive profession, and she does it with humor and inspiration. She has been in the rooms that have demanded her best. You just can't get better advice! ~ **Casey Kramer, Actress, *Behind the Candelabra, Dexter, Southland, The Young & the Restless***

Bev Leech is my most trusted referral source for new talent. Her clients are always prepared, crafted, and ready to work. ~ **Michael Colucci, Producer/Manager/Writer**

Anyone interested in pursuing a career in acting could benefit from the detailed information she provides. Sharing her wealth of experience and knowledge, Leech is both encouraging and pragmatic. ~ **Publishers Weekly**

Bev Leech is a fine actress and a top-notch teacher. Her book includes all the tips and tricks and do's and don'ts that actors really need in this business. ~ **Val Jobara, Actor, *Rush, Kickass, The Bronx Is Burning***

Through candid words of wisdom and with a remarkable luminosity, Beverly shines a beacon of light on the business of acting. ~ **Kenneth Noel Mitchell, Head of Acting: New Studio/Tisch NYU; Guthrie Theatre**

Beverly Leech has done a masterful job of moving the reader from the beginning of their journey as an actor to the audition. You will not find a better resource for the business side of acting - a "must read." ~ **Joe Montague, *Riveting Riffs Magazine***

I've come across very few artists as passionate and devoted to the pure craft of acting as Bev. She is such an amazing person to have in your artistic circle. ~ **Amanda Moresco, Writer and Producer**

You're here because this book is great! ~ **Ajay Jhaveri, Argentum Photo *Headshot Cafe [Video Interview]***

ACTOR MUSCLE ™

CRAFT. GRIT. WIT.

A Professional Guide
to the Business of Acting

BEVERLY LEECH

ACTOR MUSCLE ™: **CRAFT. GRIT. WIT.**
A PROFESSIONAL GUIDE TO THE BUSINESS OF ACTING

ISBN-10: 0615705308
ISBN-13: 978-0-615-70530-9

Cover photos by Denise Duff
Cover and book design by Kelly Andersson
Proofreader and updates by Amy Bowker

CONTENTS

INTRODUCTION

I was hoofing in the trenches of Regional summer stock when I got a call from my agent – a talent scout from Los Angeles was taking appointments for new faces. She gave me the time and place, told me to bring two contrasting monologues, and be ready to put it to tape. At the time, I was burning to be in New York, hopefully as a "triple threat." I drove two hours, gave my two best turns, then went back to rehearsals and promptly forgot about it. I'd had these kinds of calls before, and nothing ever came of it. With my sights on New York, I literally had a ticket in my purse, my stuff in storage, a job, and a roommate waiting for me. But you know what they say, *Make plans and the gods laugh.*

Two days before I was supposed to leave, my agent called.

"You booked it."

"Booked what?" I asked.

"The job. The Talent Scout. Darling, you're going to Los Angeles." My heart bounced like a water balloon. "Wait a minute. I'm going to New York, not Los Angeles. I know nothing about L.A. or television or film." I was a theatre rat from way back and this really put a cramp in my plan. I hadn't auditioned for a specific show, it'd been just a "General" for a scout, and honestly they weren't airing that show in my neck of the woods, so I wasn't at all familiar with it. After several phone calls and haggling, she convinced me to delay my flight for a couple of weeks, do the job, and then go to New York. Four months and eleven episodes later, I was still in Los Angeles, and the heat from the show had landed me two agents and an apartment. So there I was with a handful of stage credits, a couple of Regional commercials, no friends, no contacts, and no discernible skills for that market. In spite of the notoriety from the show, I felt deep down I was screwed. I had a lot of fear that I wouldn't be competitive in Los Angeles. My new agents believed in my talent, and they still do, but the business of acting does not hinge on talent alone. I had to start over, develop new relationships and new skills ... bloom where I was planted.

Back then, there were no books or classes on how to write a proper cover letter, or computers to set your resume margins: no do-this and *never*-do-that on auditions. I learned what to do by doing exactly the wrong thing. Fortunately, I'm smart, tough, and a worker bee. I simply learned as I went and I made a million mistakes. It took me a few years and rigorous reexamination to figure out how to properly conduct myself and to stay patient, flexible, and consistent in my approach to my appointments and bookings. Eventually I became a working actor.

Early in that struggle, I found a master teacher, Stella Adler, who taught me to think like a warrior – a spiritual warrior, a road warrior. One of her famous quotes was *"Life beats down and crushes your soul. Art reminds you that you have one."* I was always struck by Stella's driving desire to pass on the knowledge and experience of her master teacher, Constantin Stanislavski, to the actors who came after her. She would say, *"You're useless unless you can give it away. It's all about the work – the rest is ego and bullshit."* I think she was talking about both acting and living.

And so it goes ... I was recruited to teach at the Adler Academy in 2000 and simultaneously continued my acting career. I never thought I would teach – it never occurred to me that it would be so deeply fulfilling and add a different aspect of humility and purpose to my life. The only problem was, I saw hundreds of brilliant actors graduate with astonishing acting skills, yet they were falling through the cracks – one by one they succumbed first to failure and then to surrender. I am flooded with phone calls and letters – "I know you work. I've got all this training, but NOW what?" This was and still is a huge problem across every campus where I've taught. Everything is focused on the actor's instrument with no attention on finding an agent, getting an audition, or even writing a resume, never mind how actors should properly conduct themselves once they get an appointment. I've witnessed a lot of "professional suicide" by actors who stubbornly clung to faulty execution of inappropriate material in an audition setting.

Actors by nature are renegades. We don't want to conform – we want to act and that's all. We walk a fine line between self-delusion and inspiration. We'll plunge to dangerous depths for psychological menace in a role, but mew like a stray cat over a cold call to an agent. If all you want is a great hobby, then keep your day job and join a theatre company on the weekends. But if you want to make a living at it, you have to embrace the hard truth that you have to use all aspects of your instrument. Not just your heart and soul and senses, and only one part of your brain. You have to use both sides of your brain – the right and the left, the creative and the practical – in order to succeed. You have to face the fact that you won't pay the rent with your artistry, unless you put in the time and effort to organize your portfolio and streamline your interview techniques toward a professionally thoughtful and businesslike presentation. You don't get to do one without the other.

While teaching business skills to actors over the years, I came to another realization. The devil is in the details. A lot of acting texts are beautifully written and quite accurate in facts, but they seemed to talk "about" the business, and not really how to execute it. Much of my time over the years was spent accumulating materials and designing coursework outside of the texts that showed my students how to actually apply their actor muscle "in the rooms." Many years and a dozen teaching binders later, I'm sharing my materials with you. This is a resource guide to the Los Angeles market and beyond; a "how to" manual on the business of acting from one professional to the next generation of young bloods.

Whether you are a new or established professional, a teacher or student, in transition from theatre to film, or another state, this book is for you. Chapter One is geared for the brand-new hopeful, the rank beginner who burns with the flame but hasn't focused that desire into do-able actions. It can also be helpful to the seasoned actor in the midst of a category transition prompted by age or physical changes, those who want to re-evaluate their place in the industry. Beyond that, all chapters will be useful no matter where you are on the road. Chapter Two is about the portfolio, and I've attempted to stay current with the up-to-date practices and services of largely the West Coast market. With modest adjustments, they can be applied to the East Coast and regional markets. The resources listed are either solid referrals from working actors and agents, or those I've used myself with good results. Absolutely none of those mentioned have paid for placement in this book – either directly or indirectly. They are listed because I honestly believe they are useful and legitimate.

Detailed chapters include step-by-step actions for clean executions of auditions for stage, television and film (including commercials.) They are based on 30 years of experience and I've pretty much done it all: Broadway, series commitments, guest stars, regional theatre, national commercials, industrials, cabaret, and variety. I must be doing something right, because I'm still booking. There are many other books available that focus on business skills in specialty markets – commercials, voice-overs, and agency interviews. I don't believe this is the only book you will need, but I do believe it provides a solid and legitimate foundation of professional taste and insight. Not all my chapters are entertaining – some are just straightforward information, because I want you to get busy yesterday. I've seasoned it, though, with a little sugar of wit, and a little salt of tales in the trenches to help you learn from others' mistakes ... including my own.

I cannot promise you a career, but I can show you the path toward a career worth having. I am circumspect when I read the urgent ads for "secrets" and "shortcuts" to getting an audition or the big break. I share the discouragement and heartbreak of the young actors who lunged at shallow opportunities or paid far too much for a service or job, only to be robbed of their safety, their savings, and their dignity. I see the celebrity status of newcomers and I know it's all smoke and mirrors because I've been there myself. The public sees only an easy road, but the actor, the working actor, knows it comes at a price – and there is always a heavy price, eventually, for fame. The "worker bees" without the celebrity status know that it's about the hard work that ensures their longevity. The purpose of this book is to help young hopefuls reach for legitimate skills and services that will support the challenging privilege of building an acting career; to consistently find work in this industry, through all of its ever-changing tastes; to survive its "feast or famine" and "crickets or cannonballs" energy.

Experience. You either have your own, or you witness and learn from others. Don't strive to "make it," just strive to pave your own road and walk it like a warrior. Take courage from an old stage wisdom: *Fame is what others give you; success is what you give yourself.*

CHAPTER 1

SELF-AWARENESS, GOALS, AND THE GAME PLAN

SELF-AWARENESS

IT'S NOT PERSONAL

The biggest lesson I've learned about the acting business is: it's not personal ... none of it. But I have the responsibility to address myself personally to becoming the kind of actress and individual who can compete in the market. As an artist, I need talent and imagination; as a marketable actor, I need training, personality, experience, and tenacity. In combination, I will also need the help of good information, business contacts, preparation, and a little bit of luck. As a person, however, I need to develop endurance – and a kind of freedom from my insecurities, weaknesses, and inhibitions that block the path of achievement in my career.

Looking back, there were no shortcuts to my development. It was a simple recurring path: Awareness to Acceptance to Action. If I skipped any part of this process, like being aware, then diving immediately into action without the acceptance, then the negative experience would repeat itself and I would have to start again. Awareness and acceptance come first, and are key to successfully engaging in the action I need to develop to become a better person and a better actor.

First, acknowledge who you are, right now at this moment, and build from there. Does anybody really know exactly who they are or what they want? Most don't, but you know enough. If you are suffering from an inner critic, then please note at the top of your assets: Human Being. That means you are fallible, and make mistakes, but also have a capacity for wonder and adaptability. Try to frame yourself within a context of accepting yourself as a work in progress, a person whose job is not to be perfect, *but to be continuously evolving.*

Perfectionism is nothing but a set-up for failure because perfection is not possible. Not in this world, not in this lifetime. Change is inevitable, and if you're passionate, those changes can lead to excellence. Strive for excellence, not perfection. The key to change and shaping your own journey is a learning curve that starts with Awareness to Acceptance and then to Action. Acceptance is not surrender; it is maturity. Here's an example of how that worked for me:

Woody Allen once said, *"Ninety percent of success is just showing up."* At 20-something, I knew that I had a decent, even passable, singing voice (Awareness), but honestly, I was weak in training and not competitive (Acceptance.) My long-term goal was to perform on Broadway as a triple threat: acting, singing and dancing. So I showed up (Action) for the singing lessons (short-term goal.)

Showing up isn't just about showing up for the audition. It's about showing up for yourself.

THE INNER CRITIC

"Good Dog, Bad Dog" is an inner struggle that exists for most every person, a fight between a good dog on one shoulder and a bad dog on the other. The good dog says, "You're wonderful, precious, I believe in you, and keep up the good work." The bad dog says, "You're stupid, worthless, and hopeless, without talent – just quit already!" All day long, there's a dogfight, each dog barking at the other. Who wins? The one you feed. Feed the good dog.

Every artist plagued by their dark side should read a small but mighty booklet called *Owning Your Own Shadow: Understanding the Dark Side of the Psyche* by Robert A. Johnson. It helped me understand and accept my artistic duality: that however high the brilliance shines, there co-exists a shadow, equal in depth and darkness. Both must be embraced as part of the whole.

CLARIFYING STRENGTHS AND WEAKNESSES

Part of shaping your career is starting with examining where you are right now. Before you start this exercise, remember: in this world, there will always be someone smarter than you, and dumber than you; better looking than you, and homelier; more talented, and less talented, and sometimes even a complete fraud. Stand tall in the position that you are what you are, where you are right now, and in the right and perfect place at this moment. As an exercise, write down your personal strengths and weaknesses, and then your talent-based strengths and weaknesses. Be honest, but not brutal. State everything with simplicity, including traumatic or graphic life events. You have an opportunity to make something of yourself, and even survive yourself in order to stay in the game.

The assets are there to remind you that nobody is "all bad." Liabilities are not "bad" and they are not "wrong" - they either work for you or they don't. Liabilities will get in the way of becoming an actor, and you can do something about them. Besides, through some universal twist of irony, you will learn in time that some of your assets will become liabilities, and some of your liabilities will become assets. Not all things can be, nor should be, explored in an acting class – if you need outside help, get it! The most important thing is to see yourself clearly without tearing yourself to pieces.

Remember, "it's not personal," so keep this simple. In the upcoming table are some examples of common problems/abilities that actors possess when they're starting out. After reading through the following examples, make out a worksheet with your own personal and talent-based strengths and weaknesses.

Personal Strengths	**Personal Weaknesses**
Good sense of humor	Moody
Honest, willing	Very shy
Hard-working	Self-critical, self-loathing
Athletic	Painful childhood
On time, punctual	Drinks too much
Helpful	Sloppy
Good student	Money problems

Acting Strengths	**Acting Weaknesses**
Good looks	Crooked teeth
Talented	Poor speaking voice/accent
Poetic, sensitive	Can't express emotions
Ambitious	Stage fright, freezes up
Good with comedy	Can forget deadlines
Singing voice	Clumsy or awkward
Good with dialects	Unprepared with material
Loves Chekhov	Needs more training

If lists aren't your thing, many actors find journaling, or writing a private letter to themselves, very helpful. Whatever it takes to be clear, simple, and honest will work.

For those concerned or doubtful about physical or genetic disabilities interfering with their ability to succeed, there's more information in the additional section later in this chapter, "What's Your Excuse?"

GOALS

The next part of the exercise is to write down what you see yourself doing with your skills as an actor and in which medium(s) you'd prefer (stage, television, film, etc.) This is not about where you are right now, this is about the near and distant future – the dreams and aspirations you have. If you can see it, and paint the details in your mind's eye, then you can plan for it.

Don't bog yourself down with "I don't know if it's _____." Or "I can't _____!" Say instead, "If I knew I could do this and not fail, I would _____."

Stick to highly specific goals, and avoid broad, random statements like "be a star." Examples are: series regular on a television show; make independent films in the following genres: _____; work with (Director), (Writer); do stand-up comedy at _____; write a web series; get a commercial agent and book regional and national commercials; summer stock with Shakespeare Regional Company. The possibilities are endless, and clarity of mind is key – what do you see in your mind's eye? If you haven't got an idea, begin now.

If you knew you could do this and not fail, what would you do?

Don't fool yourself into thinking this isn't important. One day you will have an agency meeting or lunch with a potential manager, and they'll surprise you with a question like "Where do you see yourself in a year?" or "What do you think you can accomplish in five years?" This kind of questioning happens every day. An agent wants a client who knows who they are and what they want, with a plan that's grounded with do-able activity. In the meantime, you need the focus and determination of a self-starter, instead of just waiting to be discovered.

WORK THROUGH OBSTACLES, PUT GOALS INTO ACTION

To give your goals shape and forward movement, think about any liabilities and which obstacles keep you from moving forward. Then, address the steps and actions you can take toward overcoming these blocks. For example:

"I see myself as a triple threat on Broadway." Then I look at my strengths and weaknesses list. I see that I have a passable voice, but not strong enough to compete in New York. I have strong acting training, and I'm a great dancer – so, two out of three. I look for good singing coaches, start training, and practice every day.

"I have great talent, but suffer from depression or childhood trauma." (Yes, emotional instability will impede your ability to gain and hold employment.) Then the next step is to seek therapy and counseling.

"I have a drinking problem." One might then consider a 12-step program.

"I see myself as a Leading Lady and a film actress." The personal weakness might be bad teeth, which would show up on the big screen. The next logical plan is to start saving toward braces; or the liability might be "I don't have film credits to get an agent." The next step is to build credits by self-submitting for films, starting in smaller supporting roles and building to larger roles, and developing a good reputation. The reel clips from these projects will help get a better agent with more business relationships to casting and production creatives.

"Work in America." Liability? Work/Visa papers not in order. Possible plan? Start saving money for an immigration attorney – there's a referral list in a later chapter under "Legal Resources." Or, get yourself cast in a film with a studio that's willing to take on your Visa process.

WHY CLARITY AND GOALS ARE IMPORTANT

TRUE STORY: Once upon a time, I was just another unseasoned, small-town girl from the Midwest, but I had a strong commitment to my goals. I seriously wanted to be a triple threat on Broadway. I'd done some regional theatre and commercial work and I knew I could continue to work in those markets. I could also see myself as a series regular on a television series – and doing film. I wanted to be a character actress, not just another pretty girl. My mind's eye saw everything, from mid-scene under proscenium lights to "last looks" before a take. I don't know where those pictures came from, but they were specific down to the threads. One day, very soon after my move to Los Angeles, I was blown away by a phone call from an agent (let's call him Big Daddy) at a very big, very powerful agency (let's call them Big Dick Agency.)

Well, Big Daddy at Big Dick Agency had seen me on TV and wanted an interview for possible representation. I was exhilarated and terrified; overwhelmed that such a big agency would be interested in a newcomer. Admittedly, I had no real interview skills, and I probably stuttered and clucked.

After a quick but amiable question and answer session, Big Daddy sent me down the hall with his assistant to sign with the Big Dick Agency. The assistant, however, was not quite as enthusiastic – she was jaded, sarcastic, and tired from a long day in the trenches. She slapped down a contract, showed me where to sign, and huffed back to her desk. I began to read the contract – and this really ticked her off.

"What are you doing?"

"I'm reading the contract."

"Why?"

"I never sign anything without reading it first."

"Honey, this is Big Dick Agency. You're lucky to be in the building."

(Beat)

"Okay. But I'm still going to read the contract."

(Echoed tightly) "Okay. But I'm still going to leave in ten minutes. You have ten minutes."

I continue reading and I see the language "Soap Opera" throughout. I'm confused. I don't recall any discussion that representation was exclusively for Daytime (Soaps.) And there is no mention of television, film, commercials, or stage in the contract. At my peril, I gently query:

"This contract is to do only soaps?"

"That's right."

"What about television and film? I want to do theatre in New York ... "

(She snorts, cutting me off) "No. No. We don't really see you doing that."

"At all?"

"At all. Ever."

"Will I be able to interview with another department in the agency in order to do that?"

(With deadly intent) "Honey, this is Big Dick. This is all you're ever gonna get."

I tore up the contract, then went home and threw up. Later, I signed with a different agency – people who saw me the same way I did. Within a year, I booked guest star spots, then a television series. I did Broadway, too. I worked in films, national commercials ... *and* soaps.

Back then, the market was more strident – you couldn't act your way out of a soap contract. Once a soap actress, always a soap actress. There's nothing wrong with that work. In fact, it's very challenging and I have a lot of respect for my friends who do it. I just didn't want to be limited or mocked by a snark that decreed I wasn't good enough to want more. Some actors are so scared and so eager to "make it" that they'll take whatever is in front of them. I'm not psychic and I don't gamble, so at the time, I couldn't really predict whether I was on the right path. But I believed I knew who I was and who I could be. I didn't betray myself. I simply coupled my personal strengths (intelligence, self-discipline, and a strong work ethic) with a liability (yep, my stubbornness is now an asset) and put them into play. As soon as possible, I began to study with master teachers, wised up, and rehearsed every day to achieve the competitive edge I would need.

This is for you, actors: See it. Do it. Be it.

THE GAME PLAN

ACTING ISN'T ONE BIG DECISION, IT'S ONE LONG DECISION.

Give yourself a window of time: at least five years. It takes about a year and a half of consistent effort to break in, and maybe another few to quit your day job. *If you fail to plan, then you are planning to fail.* Below is a reasonable and orderly path for any new actor.

SAMPLE GAME PLAN for an actor in Los Angeles, early stages (1-5 years), and/or new in town. Your current resume is a handful of theatre credits, zero to minimal TV/Film, and maybe a handful of webisodes. Your goal: consistent work in TV/Film.

1. Establish a home base in Los Angeles

   - Good survival job – having a part-time job IS being a working actor

   - Meet transportation needs – car, metro

   - Communication – cellphone, computer, internet access, and printing services (or home printer)

2. Portfolio

- Headshots – photo session, print two looks minimum (100 copies each)

- Update resume to current market. (Chapter 2 reviews the layout for the LA/NYC market)

3. List yourself online. Join either Breakdown Services' Actors Access, Casting Networks, Now Casting, Casting Frontier, and/or Backstage.

4. Simultaneously find an agent while building your resume. Most agents won't take a meeting if you don't have a reel, if your resume isn't strong, and if you don't have a Union card.

5. Begin now with self-submissions for projects and roles that will consider newcomers. These will build your resume to help you get a decent agent. Projects can be found on the breakdowns listed with the online casting sites noted above.

6. Join the Actors' Union(s) when you are eligible.

7. Rinse and repeat. Below are brief explanations of these steps, and are broken down even further with step-by-step instructions in the next chapters

BUILD YOUR RESUME

In the beginning, go after smaller roles and Co-Stars in all markets with the intention of building into larger ones: Guest Star, Supporting Leads, and Leads. Submit to both Union and Non-Union until you get your cards. Here's how to do this across the following mediums:

THEATRE

Audition for both Union and Non-Union (Equity Waiver, Regional, and League Auditions.) If booked and the show is good, paper the city with invitations to Casting, and carefully chosen agents and managers to encourage them to attend – use it as your showcase. If an Equity production, get your voucher toward your card. Even if you don't plan to be a stage actor, join AEA – it's the "sister union" to SAG-AFTRA and can be helpful in joining those unions as well. Don't avoid theatre; many industry people respect these credits as it's a sign of self-discipline and staying power. My first union card was AEA. I've been brought in for television and film projects after a casting director saw me in a play. I also signed with my first good theatrical agent after she saw me on stage.

FILM

Film School projects, SAG Low Budget Films, Modified Low Budget, and Independent Films. These projects are more open to hiring a fledgling actor. Gain vouchers from any Union project toward your Union card. On non-paying gigs, negotiate for your scene clips or a copy of the movie to build your reel. Submit to both Union and Non-Union until you get your card(s.)

TELEVISION

Submit for smaller co-star parts and some web series. It's still stronger on a resume to have TV than the web series, but both dogs hunt. Do air checks for TV and/or gather links for web series. Keep track of your scenes to eventually edit a demo reel. Get vouchers if you book a Union show as a non-union talent.

FIND AN AGENT

Work on this at the same time you're building your resume. It's a series of actions, on separate fronts – mailing packages and listing online. This is explained below and in greater detail later in the book.

Order online or go to Samuel French and Drama Book Shop to pick up a current agency book, and/or *The Call Sheet* from Backstage. Research and seek out small to mid-size boutique agencies. Do not focus on big agencies; they will not see newcomers without credits or current earning power. Choose eight to ten agencies that sound promising, then double-check their client's credits on IMDb Pro to see if they're booking the types of projects you're keen to do. Then send "a package" in the mail: cover letter, headshot, and resume (and a demo reel or link if you have it.) If they have an email available, send both electronic and hardcopy of your materials. Some state their preference in the agency books, so comply with their requests. Repeat this process with another eight to ten new choices every couple of weeks. If you can't find an agent, get a manager who develops new talent. Submit your package to them in the same manner.

Actors Access offers Talent Link, and Casting Networks offers Talent Scout. Both of these allow a non-represented subscriber of their site to join this digital pool of actors seeking representation. Agents and managers visit these sites on the lookout for new faces and new talent. The *basic* accounts are free; these extra services are not, but they are affordable.

Agency Showcases are another way to go, but expensive and replete with scams. Research them to see if they're bonded on the DLSE website; check their credentials in the agency books you've purchased; or research them on IMDb Pro. If they're established and legitimate and you have the money, it's your call.

Continue to self-submit to casting directors, until you get representation. Once you sign with an agent/manager, they will take over with casting submissions. However, you can always continue to introduce yourself to new casting rooms, or remind established casting contacts, by sending a package or postcard, or marketing materials promoting your current play or booking.

DEVELOP AND EDIT A REEL

Take any good material garnered from your bookings on self-submissions and invest in a good editor for a reel. Student films, non-union projects, webisodes, and Union low-budget films are excellent sources of material in the beginning stages – you just want to make sure that the picture and audio quality are solid before you use them in a reel. Bad camera work/lighting and hissing audio will not invite interest in you. Systematically send your reel/links to agents and casting directors, either by mail or email, until you get some heat. You can host your demo online with any of the casting sites you're with, either as a full reel or in separate clips to target specific role types and projects. The length of the full reel should be no longer than four to five minutes, and you should limit the timing of individual clips from 25 seconds to one minute. You just want to give them a taste of your range and abilities – and honestly that's all they really ask for anyway – so don't push a lengthy reel on them.

NEVER NEGLECT YOUR TRAINING

Every good actor needs technique and scene study. Start with that, and then go after your specialties one at a time. Actors can learn camera technique in a class or workshop, or learn on their feet when they book a project. If commercials are of interest to you, take a commercial workshop. If soap operas are of interest, take that workshop. But always ground yourself in a good, basic acting technique; it will sustain you, and it can be shifted in energy to accommodate any medium (film, TV, commercials, soaps, stage.)

You are competing against others who are trained, so get some muscle to stay in the game. Be wary of "aficionados" who proclaim that technique and methods will kill your natural instinct – they've usually become jaded by a bad experience and simply haven't studied with the right people. Training didn't kill "me", it made me a better "me" and enlarged the inner size of my creative instrument.

"Energy breeds energy" says a law of physics. The habits and discipline of study will give you lots to do during the hiatus between casting seasons. When the next season begins, you'll have more in your tool belt to offer.

JOIN THE ACTORS' UNIONS

Somewhere along the path above, you may have the opportunity to join one of the actors' unions: SAG-AFTRA, and AEA. Do so when the time is right for you. Non-union talent are considered amateurs, and a union card is the sign of a professional. This is also true in the eyes of most agents, as they predominantly submit to union-status projects. I had great difficulty signing with a good agency until I had my union cards.

Non-union actors may submit themselves for both union and non-union projects. Once union, however, a union talent may not do non-union projects. However, the unions have many, many flexible contracts and provisions for their members on low-budget projects. There is still plenty of work to be enjoyed by both union and non-union hopefuls.

OTHER MARKETS TO CONSIDER - New York

The above is a sample plan for those engaged in the Los Angeles market whose priority is mostly on television and film, and perhaps stage. If your priority, however, is being a New York-based actor, many of the same principles of action apply, but you need to adjust resources to reflect the differences in the New York market.

In New York, it's obvious that theatre and stagecraft play a more important role – therefore, never neglect the stage. Make sure that your training will support this endeavor, as most production creatives in New York will not respect you without it. In Los Angeles, stagecraft seems to be lower on the list; in New York it's at the top of the list.

Therefore you should assertively audition for regional theatre companies in addition to local productions. The circuit of artistic directors is small, and your good reputation in a sound regional company production is respected and paid forward. It is the actor's best training ground for Broadway.

The commercial and soap opera markets are also very strong in New York, and television and film production are populated with the elite. Educate yourself on the pace, taste, style, and genre of each New York production, in order to polish and adapt your delivery.

In Los Angeles, agency contracts are exclusive. In New York, however, if you don't sign an exclusive contract, you are free to sign with more than one agent. Then they compete against each other to get you in the room. A good goal is to find a strong bi-coastal agency that can easily submit you on both coasts.

Resumes: Adjust the order of the credits on your resume to reflect the taste and expectation of the coast you are working. In Los Angeles, the resumes begin with film and television. In New York, they begin with theatre and film, or film and theatre – lead with whichever category has your most impressive credits.

Only the best of the best truly energize the New York market. Your craft and training must be keenly attended to and honed to excellence and sophistication. Do not neglect your training and rehearse it daily on your own.

WHAT'S YOUR EXCUSE?

As actors, we survive many of life's intrusions. And life will always intrude: death, divorce, bankruptcy, drug and alcohol addictions, car accidents, breakups, poverty, illness, even "Acts of God" including tornados and hurricanes. Part of living a fulsome human experience is failure, taboo, and setbacks – and we cannot allow ourselves to use these as excuses to prevent us from pursuing our careers. It's not about the fall, it's about getting up. But what if the setback is genetic or biological?

The website disabled-world.com has listings that reveal famous and inspirational figures born with an incredible range of conditions and illnesses, who managed to succeed in spite of it. They come from all walks of life, worked in nearly every trade and profession, and dealt with conditions such as: Mood Disorders – Tourette's Syndrome – Cerebral Palsy – Epilepsy – Dyslexia (ADD, etc.) – Obsessive Compulsive Disorder (OCD) – Hearing Impairments – ALS (Lou Gehrig's Disease) – Club Foot – Stuttering –Parkinson's – Asperger's – and many other challenging disabilities.

If you see that others have gone before you with the same problems, and even bigger problems, you may be encouraged to listen to the beating of your heart and pursue your talents and gifts. Visit this website and let these pioneers amaze you so that you can amaze yourself. Many of those listed below, living prior to the early 1900's, are suspected to have had Attention Deficit Disorder (ADD) based on the research of available public records, and study of their personal lives, and personality traits.

PEOPLE WITH ATTENTION DEFICIT DISORDER (ADD)[1]

ARCHITECT
Frank Lloyd Wright (1867-1959)

ARTISTS
August Rodin (1840-1917)
Salvador Dali (1904-1989)
Pablo Picasso (1882-1973)
Vincent Van Gogh (1853-1890) .
Leonardo Da Vinci (1452-1519)

ATHLETES
Terry Bradshaw (1948-Present) Quarterback
Babe Ruth (1895-1948) Baseball

---

[1] *Reprinted with the permission of Disabled-World.com*

Bruce Jenner (1949-Present) Track and Field
Carl Lewis (1961-Present) Olympic Gold Track and Field
Greg Louganis (1960-Present) Olympic Gold Diver
Magic Johnson (1959-Present) Basketball
Michael Jordan (1963-Present) Basketball
Nolan Ryan (1947-Present) Baseball
Jason Kidd (1973-Present) Basketball
Michael Phelps (1985-Present) Olympic Gold Swimmer
Pete Rose (1941-Present) Baseball
Alberto Tomba (1966-Present) Alpine Skier

AUTHORS
Agatha Christie (1890-1976)
Charlotte & Emily Bronte, (1816-1854 and 1818-1848)
Edgar Allan Poe (1809-1849)
Ernest Hemingway (1899-1961)
F. Scott Fitzgerald (1896-1940)
George Bernard Shaw (1856-1950)
Hans Christian Anderson (1805-1875)
Henry David Thoreau (1817-1862)
Jules Verne (1828-1905)
Leo Tolstoy (1828-1910)
Lewis Carroll (1832-1898)
Samuel Johnson (1709-1784)
Mark Twain (Samuel Clemens) (1835-1910)
Emily Dickenson (1830-1886)
Ralph Waldo Emerson (1803-1882)
Virginia Woolf (1882-1941)
William Butler Yeats (1865-1939)

COMPOSERS
Wolfgang Amadeus Mozart (1756-1791)
Beethoven (1770-1827)
Georg Frederic Handel (1685-1759)

ENTREPRENEURS AND BUSINESS LEADERS
Andrew Carnegie (1835-1919) Industrialist, Philanthropist
Malcolm Forbes (1919-1990) Publisher
Henry Ford (1863-1947) Automobile Manufacturer
John D. Rockefeller (1839-1037) Industrialist, Philanthropist
F.W. Woolworth (1852-1919) Department Store Owner
Milton Hershey (1857-1945) Chocolate Confectioner
William Randolph Hearst (1863-1951) Newspaper Magnate
William Wrigley, Jr. (1933-1999) Chewing Gum

EXPLORERS
Christopher Columbus (1451-1506) Navigator, Explorer
Lewis and Clark (1804-1806) Expedition of the Pacific Northwest.
Sir Richard Francis Burton (1821-1890) Geographer, Translator, Ethnologist, Spy

ENTERTAINERS
Anne Bancroft (1931-2005) Actress
Cher (1946-Present) Actress, Singer
Danny Glover (1947-Present) Actor
Dustin Hoffman (1937-Present) Actor
Jim Carrey (1962-Present) Actor, Comedian
Steve McQueen (1920-1980) Actor
Suzanne Somers (1946-Present) Actress
Stevie Wonder (1950-Present) Singer, Musician
Tom Smothers (1937-Present) Actor, Singer
Tracy Gold (1969-Present) Actress
John Denver (1043-1997) Singer, Musician
Bill Cosby (1937-Present) Actor
George Burns (1896-1996) Actor
George C. Scott (1927-Present) Actor
Harry Belafonte (1927-Present) Actor, Singer

Henry Winkler (1945-Present) Actor, Producer
John Lennon (1940-1980) Singer, Musician
Kirk Douglas (1916-Present) Actor
Lindsay Wagner (1949-Present) Actress
Mariel Hemingway (1961-Present) Actress
Ozzy Osbourne (1948-Present) Singer
Sylvester Stallone (1946-Present) Actor
Walt Disney (1901-1971) Producer, Screenwriter,
Director, Animator
Whoopi Goldberg (1955-Present) Actress, Comedienne
Will Smith (1968-Present) Actor, Rapper
Jack Nicholson (1937-Present) Actor
Ty Pennington (1964-Present) Television Host
Elvis Presley (1935-1977) Singer, Actor
Evil And Robbie Knievel (1938-2007) Motorcycle
Daredevil Hall of Fame
Justin Timberlake (1981-Present) Singer, Actor
Robin Williams (1952-Present) Actor, Comedian

INVENTORS
Alexander Graham Bell (1847-1922) Engineer, inventor
of the telephone
Thomas Edison (1847-1931) Phonograph, Motion
Picture Camera, Lightbulb
Benjamin Franklin (1706-1790) Founding Father of the
USA. Lightning Rod, Bifocals, and the Franklin Stove

PHOTOGRAPHERS
Ansel Adams (1902-1984) Black and white photos of the
American West

PHYSICISTS
Albert Einstein (1879-1955) Quantum Theory, Theory of
Relativity

POLITICAL FIGURES

James Carville (1944-Present) Political Consultant, Pundit, Litigator

John F. Kennedy (1917-1963) U.S. President

Abraham Lincoln (1809-1865) U.S. President

Dwight D. Eisenhower (1890-1969) U.S. President, General

Eleanor Roosevelt (1844-1962) First Lady

Muhammad Anwar el-Sadat (1918-1981) Egyptian President

Napoleon Bonaparte (1769-1873) Emperor

Nelson Rockefeller (1908-1979) U.S. Vice President

Prince Charles (1948-Present) Prince of Wales

Robert F. Kennedy (1925-1968) U.S. Attorney General

Winston Churchill (1874-1065) British Prime Minister

Woodrow Wilson (1856-1924) U.S. President

SCIENCE & MEDICINE

Sir Isaac Newton (1642-1727) Mathematician, Astronomer, Physicist. The Laws of Gravity

Galileo (1564-1642) Astronomer, Mathematician

Harvey Cushing M.D. (1869-1939) Neurosurgeon

Louis Pasteur (1822-1895) Chemist. Vaccines for rabies and anthrax. Pasteurization

Nostradamus (1503-1566) Physician

Werner von Braun (1912-1977) Rocket Scientist

MILITARY FIGURES

Gen. William C. Westmoreland (1914-Present) Vietnam-era General

General George Patton (1885-1945) WWII General

Eddie Rickenbacker (1890-1973) WWI Ace

CHAPTER 2

THE PORTFOLIO

HEADSHOTS

WHAT DO YOU REALLY NEED?

TWO STRONG PHOTOS that are simple, powerful or charming, and evocative. Just contrast your looks in clothing style, appearance, and temperament.

1. "Smiler" photo – pleasant, approachable, and effortless. Basic use is for the lighter mediums such as comedy in TV/Film, and commercials. This one needs a strong "inner smile" in the eyes to support the outer smile.

2. "Theatrical" photo – more serious, grounded. Basic use is for dramatic or "straight" roles.

3. A third (optional) choice is a "Character" shot – e.g. business professional or athletic or blue collar, etc.

FINDING THE PHOTOGRAPHER

Later in this chapter is a list of photographers in L.A. compiled from actor referrals. You do not have to use it – you may also ask your agent, or use other lab and actor referrals instead. Reproductions also has an onsite library of photographers on both coasts that actors can peruse.

When using the random listing, view each website to compare the style and quality of the work. Look at how they light their subjects in natural lighting and studio light; check whether the photos have texture and whether the photographers shoot "real" people. Don't pick just one. Narrow your search to 3 to 5 choices.

You can't always learn all you need to know just by website or a phone call. Once I think I've made a choice, and before I make a deposit, I always try to meet the photographer in person. It's a quick meet-and-greet to shake hands, see their studio, and feel out their personality. A good photographer will shoot a good photo – but a great photographer will help you feel at ease to do your best work. Listen to your instincts. If there's any hint of personalities not meshing, or any surly behavior, you won't rise to the occasion. It's a waste of time and money to shoot under such circumstances. Be polite, but move on to the next photographer who best fits your budget and style.

Discuss shooting indoors or outdoor shooting, and address your skin tone, age and hair coloring; talk about how to contrast backgrounds. Generally speaking, try to book your outdoor shoots at midmorning or mid-afternoon when the shade and lighting give better evenness to your face. The sun is high and hot at noontime, causing unnatural shadows and a glare that makes you squint, or sweat, or mess up your hair and makeup. Some photographers will still shoot at high noon but diffuse the lighting by placing their subjects in a cool, shady space or use screens and "kick" boards to bounce and balance the light. Indoor studio shoots give greater control over consistent light sources.

QUESTIONS TO ASK

1. Rates and what is included with that rate.

2. Usual length of time needed for the shoot.

3. How many "looks" the photographer will shoot for that rate. Do they prefer to choose the wardrobe or let you decide?

4. Film or digital? If film, some photographers ask that you use their favorite labs to process the contact sheets, and they'll offer you only a small number of 8x10 prints for you to choose; others will give you the film and you find your own lab and choose the quantity of photos. Most, however, are now shooting digitally. This means the session times are shorter, they delete unusable photos as they go, and the turnaround time is very quick – they simply download your complete session to a disc or upload images to an online site for you to review. Always ask for a master copy of the session on a disc.

5. What is the turnaround time – when will you have your images after the shoot?

6. How far in advance do you need to schedule a session?

7. Is there a deposit required? Or a cancellation fee?

8. If shooting to film, who owns the negatives?

Affordable is good, but not always better. In a perfect world, we find fabulous and affordable, but we're all on a budget and must make hard choices. Sometimes, however, spending an extra $100 on a good photographer can save you a lot of money in the end with less retouching, web enhancement, and color correction before you go to print.

If you are in your mid-20s and the quality of the photos is good, you won't need to update your photos more often than every two years, because you just won't age very much. If the actor is a youth, or older than 35, the aging process is more rapid and photos should be updated more often. Many actors – of all ages – choose to reshoot every year.

Always reshoot if you drastically change your look – hair color change, short hair cut from long (and vice versa), shaving your head, to a beard from clean-shaven, going to Punk from Midwestern, weight gain or loss, etc. It upsets casting directors and agents to request someone based on their photo, and then have a different person walk in the door. You can lose a good business contact as a result. However, you do not have to reshoot if your change is the result of a role you are playing and you plan to return to your previous look.

Plan your budget to include the post production, too. There's more to spend in processing, printing, and submissions, so don't blow your savings on the fabulous photographer if you can't afford to follow through.

PREPARING FOR THE SHOOT

CARE FOR YOURSELF

You need stamina to maintain charisma and focus. The week before a photography session, drink a lot of water, eliminate drug/alcohol consumption, get enough sleep, and stay out of the sun. The day of your session, do not arrive on an empty stomach – eat a light and delicious meal. Anything too heavy, like a steak, will make you sleepy during the shoot. Give yourself ample time to arrive punctually – lateness makes the actor stressed and this will read in the lens.

CLOTHING

Watch the current shows and ads running on television. Look for your age type, and the kinds of roles played and the clothing they wear. Think about how you would be cast for soaps, commercial, film, stage, television. Find 3 to 6 simple outfits (focus on the waist up and the close-up.) Remember: most good ideas are simple, so pay attention to the tones, colors, textures, and backgrounds.

Your face is the most important thing in the shot. You can actually be upstaged by your clothing, so stay away from chunky earrings, funky ties, wild/bold/splashy patterns, high contrast prints, bold graphics, and neon colors. Clothing is there to frame and enhance your face, not distract from it. If people are looking at your fur-lined bustier or a tie wired to "fly in the wind," then they're not looking at your face. There's always room for ingenuity, but keep in mind you want an all-purpose headshot, not a marquis to a comedy club.

Good, solid choices for clothing in a shoot are what I call "money colors" and "framers." Money colors bring out the best in your skin tones, they make you look and feel great, and people pay you compliments. If you don't know what yours are, start now to find out. Mine are smoky teals, and blue-based reds. A good general guideline is to stay away from sweatshirt grey, khaki beige, salmon, turquoise, and neon "hot" colors – these provoke extreme ends on the response meter. One makes you look tired and washed out, the other screams for too much attention. If you just can't live without your flamingo pink blouse, then layer it with a cardigan, vest, or jacket to keep it in check. "Framers" are those colors just a few shades lighter or darker than your own skin tone. The goal is to have separation between your skin, clothing, and hair. This, coupled with a contrasting background, will "frame" your face in a way that makes it prominent. For example, I'm blonde and fair-skinned. I rarely choose cream colors because it all blends together and I end up looking like a Q-tip. As a blonde, I normally stand out well with a dark or warm background, wearing darker-colored clothing. Also consider that some colors are automatically funnier than others – black and chocolate brown might not be the best choice if you're going comedic. This note will help you with both shooting "smilers" and choosing your clothing for comedy auditions.

Choose textured fabrics. These read great on camera and lend your photo a tactile feel that people respond to well. Angora wool, cable knits, silk, leather, denim, tweed, satin, and suede are examples of good texture.

Bring contrasting looks. Overall, think of a crisp and casual look (middle class) for the smiler; a dressier upscale look for the theatrical, and a third alternative look. Above all, make your choices clean, flattering, and easy to wear.

HAIR AND MAKEUP

Many photographers offer the services of a makeup artist for an additional fee. You are not obligated to use them unless you're not very good with makeup yourself. Don't stress over blemishes; these are easily fixed by a retouch artist and often automatically done in post. As a general rule, apply makeup that enhances your looks, rather than trying to fix defects. Too much makeup is a turn-off and cannot be fixed in post.

If you need a haircut or color, have it done at least a full week in advance. Give it time to settle in (and settle down.)

Men should start "dirty" with facial hair looks (5 o'clock shadow, etc.), then shave during the session for the clean-cut look. Women should reverse that, starting with clean makeup look and then building into heavier lips and liners for the more sophisticated looks. For women, it's easier to build up than to take off, and saves time for more shots. Women should avoid metallic eye shadows, because they bounce light on the flash and you'll look like a Vegas showgirl. Unless that's what you're selling, use flat colors and mattes.

MUSIC

Feel free to ask to bring any of your favorite music to play during your session to help motivate and sustain you. If you prefer silence, don't feel obligated to work with music.

THE SHOOT

The key to good shots is this: INNER PREPARATION. It's vital. It will diminish any self-consciousness and reveal the natural essence of your individuality. What people respond to is life, spontaneity, and truthfulness. Your inner smile can make the outer smile genuine and effortless. Your inner strength is a result of your life experience and convictions.

One key to the "inner smile" is to have vivid imagery through monologues, jokes, great stories, and reminiscences prepared ahead of time. During the shoot, tell yourself these stories, and as you see them in your mind's eye, your energy will shift. Whatever you are thinking is delivered through your eyes. Select material that makes you laugh, flirt, and feel caring or warm, strong or playful (just not all at once.) You can practice this at home in your mirror, projecting your energy outward. If you do this last exercise, however, be careful that you do not judge your own performance. Just go with it.

Some actors have mastered the ability to capture the moment of being "caught." The technique is to turn away, and then suddenly look into the camera repeatedly as if you've just caught someone's eye, or accidentally run into an old friend on the street.

AFTER THE SHOOT: CHOOSING FINAL SHOTS

If you suffer from too many good choices, rejoice. Your photographer has just saved you an enormous amount of time and money. Casting directors get tired of seeing the same old photo. If I've had a particularly good photo session, I choose two or three of my strongest images to begin submissions and earmark the other favorites for later. The following year or so, instead of reshooting, I'm able to print "new" photos from the old session. My agents are happy that I'm proactive and Casting has to pause a few extra seconds to look at the new headshot. It keeps things fresh and active to offer a new look every year.

HOW TO CHOOSE FINAL SHOTS:

Preview and narrow down your choices anywhere from 10 to 35 images. If you have computer skills, view each one on your screen in full size. Eliminate any that are out of focus or badly framed, or feature half-closed eyes, a tired face, or a pinched smile. Have your final choices processed into 4x6 prints. You can do this at a lab for about $2 each, or save a little money and have them processed at a local drugstore for under 25¢ each. Viewing larger prints physically in 4x6 format is really useful in sorting through the remaining choices. There still may be additional photos that are blurred or unsuitable that you didn't see as such on the computer.

Get the 4x6 or digital favorites to your agent, manager, and friends for opinions and choices. If your agent or manager insists on going through the entire shoot, including the bad shots, let them. But remember the final choice is yours – you must be happy with how you're presenting yourself to the world, not just your representation. If you include something in that "favorite" batch that you're really unhappy with or unsure about, you may hate yourself later if someone chooses it!

Many things can be fixed by a good retouch artist before you have them printed at the lab. For blemishes, cold sores, dark circles, untamed hair, a bit of clothing askew, even bandaged fingers, a good retoucher is worth their weight in gold to improve your first impression.

For older actors, do not completely eliminate your wrinkles. You can soften them, but you need to own them. It embarrasses and angers casting to call in a 32-year-old woman from a photograph, only to discover that she looks 45 in real life.

If your photographer shoots too many photos out of focus, screws up the lighting, or even burns the negative in the lab processing – do not hesitate to insist on a re-shoot. You deserve to get your money's worth. Just base the re-shoot on the technical faults. If, however, you yourself didn't bring your "A" game and shot badly (stiff, over-the-top, bad choice of clothing, too much makeup etc.), that's not the fault of the photographer. Pick your battles.

PHOTOGRAPHERS LIST

Below is a list of headshot photographers currently working in the L.A. area, with a range of skills and rates to match your taste and budget. Check with actor-related sites or your agent for more referrals.

PHOTOGRAPHER	CONTACT
JULIE HARDISTY-MOCKETT	m4prophoto.com
DAVID MULLER	davidmullerphotography.com
PATRICK MAUS	maus-photography.com
DENNIS ARPERGIS	simplyheadshots.com
BRAD BUCKMAN	bradbuckman.com
DAPPER PHOTOGRAPHY	dapperphotography.com
ROBERT DOUGLAS	robertdouglasphotography.com
PAUL SMITH	paulsmithphotography.com
KELSEY EDWARDS	kelseyedwardsphoto.com
ALAN WEISSMAN	alanweissman.com
JOAN LAUREN	joanlauren.com
MAXIMO	maximophotography.com
ADRIEN McKECHNIE	adrienphoto.com
DANA PATRICK	danapatrick.com
VANIE POYEY	poyeyphotos.com
THEO & JULIET	theoandjuliet.com
PETER KONERKO	peterkonerko.com
GEOFFREY WADE	gwheadshots.com
DICK WIEAND	dickwphoto.com
DAVID ZAUGH PHOTOGRAPHY	zaughphotography.com
DENISE DUFF	duffimages.com
KENNETH DOLIN	kennethdolin.com
KEVIN MCINTYRE	kevinmcphotograph.com
KEVYN MAJOR HOWARD	headshot-photography.com
DAVID NOLES	davidnoles.com
HILARY JONES	hilaryjones.org
KRIS KORN	k2foto.com
JEFF LORCH	jefflorch.com
PATRICK MCELHENNEY	patmackphotography.com
BRIDGE MIHALIK	bridgemihalik.com
BECKWITH PHOTOGRAPHY	beckwithphotography.com
JOHN ALLEN PHILLIPS	clickwestphoto.com
JANNA GIACOPPO	jannagiacoppo.com
ANTHONY MONGIELLO	anthonymongiello.com
KAT TUOHY	tuohyphotography.com

RESOURCES FOR MARKETING TOOLS AND MATERIALS

These are not endorsements, but examples of services to get you started. Check with actor-related sites or your agent for more choices.

PHOTO LABS TO PRINT/ PROCESS PICS, ZEDS, ETC.

Reproductions - reproductions.com
3499 Cahuenga Blvd. West
Los Angeles, California 90068
(888)797-7795 or (323)845-9595

Argentum Photo Lab - argentum.com
6550 Sunset Blvd.
Hollywood, California 90028
(323) 461-2775

Isgo Lepejian - isgophoto.com
257 S. Lake St.
Burbank, CA 91502
(818) 848-9001

New Image Prints - newimagegraphic.com
7109 W. Sunset Blvd.
Los Angeles, California 90046
(323)876-1102

Universal Print and Copy - universalprintandcopy.com
3535 Cahuenga Blvd. West
Los Angeles, California 90068
(323)876-3500

RETOUCHING

Sam Tabrizi – digitalheadshotretouching.com

Ray the Retoucher - raysphotolab.com

Also provided at Reproductions, Argentum, and Isgo's

DEMO REELS and VIRTUAL AUDITION CLIP SERVICES

Shotgun Digital (reel assembly and editing)
1242 Crescent Heights Blvd. #201
West Hollywood CA 90046
(323)466-5589 shotgundigital.com

Speedreels (reel assembly/editing; audition/reel clips)
5225 Wilshire Blvd. Suite 410
Los Angeles CA 90036
(323)931-1712 speedreels.com

Argentum - Casting Suite (affordable Eco-Cast)
6550 Sunset Blvd.
Hollywood CA 90028
(323)461-2775 argentum.com/casting suite

Now Casting – Auditions NOW (electronic platform for
self-taped auditions)
2210 W. Olive Avenue, Suite 320
Burbank, California 91506
(818)841-7165 nowcasting.com

Archetype DVD (duplication services)
John T. Woods   archetypedvd.com

Vimeo: (free reel hosting) vimeo.com

AGENCY AND CASTING MAILOUT

DO-IT-YOURSELF MAILINGS AND PACKAGES:

CastingAbout.com (a monthly subscription from Breakdown Services) and Contacts NOW (at NOW Casting) offer access to the addresses of only those casting directors and projects currently in production. Full details of associates and assistants, green light or hiatus, and label printing are all available. This saves time and money by targeting current projects and avoiding those on hiatus or cancelled.

Samuel French, Drama Book Shop, Breakdown Services, and Casting Networks offer address labels for every single talent agency and casting director in town. If you are purposely sending wide to blanket the market, then this might be a way to go, but they don't specify if, for instance, the agency represents only hand models or stunt doubles, or if the casting office is currently on hiatus for that show. Decide according to the purpose of your mailout. These labels are free at Casting Networks if you join.

Currently, no industry email list exists, but some are provided within agency books at Samuel French, Drama Book Shop, and *The Call Sheet*. Casting Networks and Breakdown Services utilize email for electronic self-submissions, but they're often cloaked in a hyperlink, so disclosure of specific addresses here is very limited. NowCasting.com hosts additional resources for mailings, postcards, and packages.

COMPANIES THAT DO MAILINGS FOR YOU:

Padded Envelopes (for actors)
paddedenvelopesla.com

Smart Girls Productions (for actors and screenwriters)
smartg.com

THE RESUME

The biggest red flag of an "amateur" is a sloppy resume, padded in all the wrong places. Later in this section (and at ActorMuscle.com) are resume templates. Carefully review these samples, and adapt the following guidelines and suggestions before creating your own.

The first resume sample is a 3-column format, with tabs, margins, headers, and footers. Credits lead with Film and Television, which is the typical layout for the Los Angeles market. The sample posted online is a fully automated plug-in and you can begin typing your resume right away. ActorMuscle.com/3column

A second sample in the 4-column format is one that some actors prefer; this is commonly seen on the East Coast. Note the difference: it begins with a Theatre section, followed by Film. On the East Coast and other regional markets outside of Los Angeles, having strong theatre credits is highly respected and is often the lead-off point to a resume. Different market, different layout.

For the bottom section of your resume, check the "Special Skills" list within this book hosting several pages of abilities and talents. Many young actors are actually stumped by this part, not believing (or not knowing) they have more than credits to offer on a resume. This list is to help jumpstart you in listing those abilities. As a rule, you should list only the things you do very, very well. Excellence is the key.

DETAILS OF THE RESUME - OVERVIEW

Credits are usually in bold and underlined on a resume. If you don't have any credits yet under a particular header, just delete that header and move on to the next one.

FILM
TELEVISION
WEB
COMMERCIAL
THEATRE
TRAINING
    Acting
    Voice (Singing range. Dialects)
    Languages (only if you are fluent)
    Dance/Movement
    Special skills

Credits must be easy to read and understand. Standard layouts use 12-point type, and no smaller than 10-point. Be sure to double-check all spelling, punctuation, and grammar.

FILM, TELEVISION, AND THEATRE

Credits for these three mediums have a similar order and structure across the page: the name of the show in the first column; the name of the role you played in the second column; and in the third column, the name of the production company, TV network, or theatre, followed by a comma and the name of the director. Some actors prefer to list the type of role (as in lead, supporting lead, guest star, co-star, and featured) instead of the name of the character, but you should choose only one option - do not use both, as in "Alaura (Lead)".

Often the name of the production company or theatre is unwieldy and won't stay inside the third column margin, especially with the director's name. It is appropriate to abbreviate, but do so in a way that it's still recognizable. For instance: SONY, NBC, FOD – and you can use Prod. for Productions and Thtr. for Theatre.

This column can be tricky, so keep working with it. The entire credit should stay on one line.

My advice is to lead with your strong suit. You should begin each section with the most recent credit, and/or the strongest credit, and work back chronologically. Try not to use any credits older than 5 years. The test for an older credit is this: are you still cast-able in this role today?

Never lie on your resume – you will be caught. One fib negates the entire page and provokes a harsh response from the casting room. For example, in theatre, amateurs embarrassed by a small resume will sometimes attempt to pad it by naming a play and the role, when the truth is that they only worked on a scene from the play in a class. This is the kind of white lie that will truly put you in deep trouble, especially if you're asked questions about it during a casting session. Industry professionals are quite literate – they'll know instantly if you've actually worked in a full production or not. This wisdom applies to every medium, not just theatre.

Unless you are making a separate resume for Central Casting to do background work, do not list your work as an extra on an acting resume. It is not considered an acting credit. Some extras are lucky enough to get "bumped" during a shoot and given lines, or even a funny "bit" that lasts a minute or two – and then it's okay to use as an acting credit. You may not have a character name in the end titles, so list yourself on the resume in the middle column as "featured," not "cameo." Recognizable names and faces of established actors normally use the distinction of the "cameo" credit.

THE WEB SERIES AND OTHER MEDIA

We are now fully engaged in a new age of the web series. Some actors choose to put these at the bottom of their television credits, while others make a new section header labeled WEB. Reality shows, hosting gigs, and industrials can also be given separate sections, though industrials are often considered commercial credits. The placement is up to you.

COMMERCIALS

Listing these might actually be good for a young actor in the beginning if your resume is thin. It's an indication that you are working and have on-camera experience – and it's better than nothing. However, once you've built your credits and are past that stage, leave them off a "theatrical" resume, which is primarily for film, television and theatre.

Additionally, some actors pull the old "List Upon Request" ruse. If you don't have a list, then don't use that phrase. It's the kind of white lie that will undermine your credibility if you're caught. If you don't have commercial credits, then delete that section altogether and move on to the next heading.

You'll note that the 4-column format lists the commercial credits with as much information as film and television. I, however, have done a lot of commercials, so I prefer to simply list the product itself and leave out the rest. Your commercial agency often has its own template and you can ask them for their sample. Because most commercial submissions are done electronically these days, commercial resumes are a thing of the past; I rarely use hardcopy. Your credits are now online with your electronic actor page, and is automatically forwarded when submitted. However, hardcopy of theatrical resumes is still used for theatrical auditions.

THE TRAINING SECTION

There is some controversy regarding listing every single teacher you've studied with at a university or two-year program. Most students have emotional attachments and want to acknowledge their teachers, but the truth is that most of them are not recognized by the industry outside of campus. Unless the instructors are renowned, "Master" teachers, or affiliated with heavyweights like Yale, Guthrie, or Steppenwolf, it's more important to list the institution and the type of training, rather than the individual. For instance, list your training as technique, scene study, Shakespeare, commercial workshop, etc. It's also acceptable to name the type of acting "method" such as Adler, Meisner, Hagen, or others. Honestly, they don't care that Joe Blow from community college taught you "vocal production," they just care that you have a spectacular British accent or Louisiana dialect.

SPECIAL SKILLS

Special skills are the hobbies, sports, awards, and unusual abilities that give you more humor and depth as a person; they qualify you for particular needs of an acting role (such as tumbling or fencing.) As a rule, you should list only those things you do very, very well. I took two years of Spanish in high school, but that does not make me fluent or proficient. Military duty/training, weapons training, and national competitions are also okay to list in this section, but add only those skills that might lend themselves to acting roles. Some actors have worked as "Techies" – but you should not list any production crew experience whatsoever. It will work against you on an acting resume, just as words-per-minute and typing skills are needed for a secretarial position but not an acting role. Additionally, if you are physically impaired or disabled in some way, embrace it – own it. I had one student who was partially deaf, which affected both his hearing and his speech. Instead of apologizing or running away from it, at the very top of his Special Skills section he listed: "FABULOSITY: Partially Hearing Impaired." Gotta love an actor with moxie.

Cautionary note on Special Skills: Do not overload this to make up for a lack of credits. I've seen actors fill up one third of their resume with this – it's too much and looks desperate.

HEADERS AND FOOTERS

Your name should be in larger type in the center of the header of the page. The days of listing your height, weight, hair color, and eye color are mostly over, and it's really only useful if you do modeling or print work. Most of this information can already be seen in your headshot, and it's listed online with your actor page. If you still think you need "filler," then either format it as shown in the the 4 Column resume sample, or split these, two deep, on either side of the margins like this:

Height: 5'5"   **Hair: Auburn**
Weight: 140   **Eyes: Green**

Otherwise, limit the header to your name (in type larger than your credits), union affiliation (if you have one), and contact information. A phone number and email will suffice. Some actors like to use a thumbnail of their headshot to one side of their name. This can be attractive and strong if done with some taste and finesse.

Note: Do *not* list your home address. Practice basic self-preservation for cities like Los Angeles and New York. Casting offices are rather trustworthy, but the odds are that your headshot and resume could end up in a trash bin. You do not want a dumpster diver to engage in a little recreational identity theft, or surprise you with a home visit. This word of caution applies to both men and women.

In the footer, if you don't have representation, then list the link to your website, reel, or any other digital material that markets you as an actor. If you do have representation, use the footer to prominently display the company name, address, and contact information, then follow it with your website if there's room. Once signed to an agent or manager, remove your personal contact information. All calls should go through them.

Examine the 3-column and 4-column resume samples I have provided below. Use them to create your own. Check the products page at actormuscle.com for the free, downloadable, automated 3-column template. One can spent hours formatting lining up columns and margins, whereas with this template you can just type in your credits. You can also change the font and point size to your taste. The 4-column resume is also available on the website as a printable viewing sample. The 4-column leads with theatre, and is commonly seen on the East Coast but many L.A. actors use the 4-column format, and lead with film. Remember, different market, different layout.

YOUR NAME HERE

UNION AFFILIATIONS HERE

Contact: 000-000-0000 | Email Address Here

FILM

Project Title	Name/Type of Role	Studio, Director
Project Title	Name/Type of Role	Studio, Director
Project Title	Name/Type of Role	Studio, Director

TELEVISION

Show Title	Type of Role	Prod Co., Director
Show Title	Type of Role	Production Co., Dir.
Show Title	Type of Role	Production Co., Dir.

THEATRE

Play Title	Type of Role/Character	Thtr Name, Director
Play Title	Type of Role/Character	Theatre Name, Dir.
Play Title	Type of Role/Character	Theatre Name, Dir.

COMMERCIALS

Name of the Product or Company
(Delete this section if you have no commercial credits)

TRAINING

ACTING:
VOICE: Range: Dialects:
LANGUAGES: (If applicable, examples: fluent or conversational French & Spanish)
DANCE/MOVEMENT: (Examples: Ballet, Tap, Ballroom, Yoga, Tai-Chi
SPECIAL SKILLS: (Examples: Weapons, Stunt driving, Gymnastic, Juggling, Impressions,
Stand-up Comedy, Piano, Golf, Horseback Riding, Fencing)

YourWebsiteHere.com

(Agency/Manager address and contact info here when you sign
and you will then delete personal contact info in the header above)

Christian Meoli

SAG-AFTRA, AEA
christianmeoli.com
5'11" – 180 lbs – Hair: Dk. Brown – Eyes: Dk. Brown – Vocal Range: High Baritone

THEATRE (Partial List)

OCTOMOM! THE MUSICAL	Doctor	Cabaret Voltaire	Christian Meoli
LOVEWATER	Benjamin	Ensemble Studio Thtr.	Jessica Kubznasky
THE DADAISTS	Playwright	The Met Theatre	Harris Mann
ABSOLUTION	Peter	Hyperion Prod, Court Thtr.	Willard Carroll
REEFER MADNESS	Jimmy	Hudson Theatre	Andy Fickman
CABARET VOLTAIRE	Producer	Steve Allen Theatre	Christian Meoli
SKY'S END	Tommy	Blank Theatre	Daniel Henning
TONY & TINA'S WEDDING	Donnie Dolce	Baltimore/D.C. Co.	Larry Pelligrini

FILM (Partial List)

TREACHERY	Supporting	Blancbiehn/Pegasus/Murphy	Travis Romero
SHOULD'VE BEEN ROMEO	Supporting	Phillybrook Films	Mark Bennett
THE LOW LIFE	Lead	Autumn Pictures	George Hickenlooper
WANDERLUST	Lead	Damaged Californians	P. James Keitel
APOCALYPSE . . . DORIS	Lead	Starving Films	Victor Goss
FINAL APPROACH	Supporting	Levinson/RHI Ent.	Armand Mastroanni
LOOKING FOR JIMMY	Supporting	Dune/Star 69	Julie Delpy
TUESDAYS WITH MORRIE	Supporting	Harpo/Carlton America	Mick Jackson
SONG OF THE LARK	Supporting	Paramount	Karen Arthur
BONGWATER	Supporting	Alliance Independent	Richard Sears
PERSONS UNKNOWN	Lead	Promark Ent/Spectator Films	George Hickenlooper
ALIVE	Lead	Kennedy/Marshall	Frank Marshall

TELEVISION (Partial List)

RAY DONOVAN (Pilot)	Guest Star	SHO	Allen Coulter
DESPERATE HOUSEWIVES	Co-Star	ABC	Ron Underwood
DOLLHOUSE	Recurring	FOX	Joss Whedon
IN PLAIN SIGHT	Guest Star	USA	Jesus Trevino
ELI STONE	Co-Star	ABC	Perry Lang
LIFE	Guest Star	NBC	Tony Wharmby
COLD CASE	Guest Star	CBS	Jim Whitmore Jr.
ALIAS	Guest Star	ABC	Robert Williams
WITHOUT A TRACE	Guest Star	CBS	Paul Halohan
NASH BRIDGES	Recurring	CBS	Carlton Cuse, EP
THE PRACTICE	Guest Star	ABC	James Patterson

COMMERCIAL (Partial List)
DELL, VOLKSWAGON, MICROSOFT, TIME/WARNER, OLYMPUS CAMERA, COORS LIGHT, MERK

EDUCATION Temple University

SPECIAL SKILLS Accents/Dialects, Sports, Improv, Harmonica, Dodgeball Leagues, Renaissance Man

Agency/Manager Name
Address and Contact Information

SPECIAL SKILLS SECTION OF THE RESUME

SPORTS
AEROBICS
ARCHERY
BADMINTON
BALLOONIST
BASEBALL
BASKETBALL
BATON TWIRLING
BILLIARDS
BOATING
BODY BUILDING
BOWLING
BOXING
CANOEING
CHEERLEADING
CRICKET
CROQUET
DIVING
FENCING
FIGURE SKATING
FISHING
FLYFISHING
FOOTBALL
FRISBEE
GOLF
GYMNASTICS
HACKEYSACK
HANDBALL
HANG GLIDING
HIKING
ICE HOCKEY
ICE SKATING
JET SKIING
JOGGING
JUMP ROPE
KAYAKING
KICK BOXING
MOUNTAIN CLIMBING
PILOT A PLANE
PING PONG
POGO STICK
RACQUETBALL
RAPPELLING
ROCK CLIMBER
ROLLER HOCKEY

ROLLER SKATING
ROLLERBLADING
RUGBY
RUNNING
SCUBA DIVING
SCULLING
SKATEBOARDING -
SKEET/TRAP SHOOTING
SKY DIVING
SNORKELING
SNOW SKIING
SNOWBOARDING
SNOWMOBILE
SOCCER
SOFTBALL
SPEED SKATING
SQUASH
SUPERCROSS
SURFING
TENNIS
TRAMPOLINE
TRAPEZE
VOLLEYBALL
WATER POLO
WATER SKIING
WEIGHT LIFTER
WINDSURFER
WRESTLING

SWIMMING
BACK STROKE
BREAST STROKE
BUTTERFLY
DIVING
FREESTYLE
SWIMMING (GENERAL)
SYNCHRONIZED

TRACK & FIELD
BROAD JUMP
DISCUS
HIGH JUMP
HURDLE
JAVELIN

LONG JUMP
MARATHON
POLE VAULT
SHOT PUT
SPRINTER
TRIATHLON

CYCLING
BMX
DOWNHILL
FLATLAND
FREESTYLE
HALF PIPE
JUMPS
MOUNTAIN BIKING
RECUMBENT
ROAD BIKING
TRIALS RIDING
UNICYCLE
VERTICAL WALL

LANGUAGES
LANGUAGES (FLUENT)
LANGUAGES (FAMILIAR)
(List all languages you can
speak fluently or passably)

DIALECTS
ARMENIAN
AUSTRALIAN
BOSTON
BRITISH
BRONX
BROOKLYN
CAJUN
CANADIAN
CHINESE
COCKNEY
FRENCH
GERMAN
IRISH
ITALIAN
JAMAICAN
JAPANESE
MANHATTAN
MEXICAN
MIDDLE EASTERN
MINNESOTA

WISCONSIN
NEW ENGLAND
PUERTO RICAN
RUSSIAN
SCANDINAVIAN
SCOTTISH
SOUTH AFRICAN
SOUTHERN
SPANISH
SWISS-GERMAN

MUSIC & DANCE

DANCE
BALLET
BALLROOM
BELLY
BREAK
CLOG
CLUB/FREESTYLE
CONTRA DANCING
DISCO
FLAMENCO
HIP HOP
HULA
IRISH DANCE
JAZZ
LINE
POINTE
POLKA
ROBOT
SALSA
SQUARE
SWING
TANGO
TAP
WALTZ

SINGING
COUNTRY
FOLK
JAZZ
MUSICAL THEATER
OPERA
POP
R&B
RAP

VOCAL RANGE
ALTO
BARITONE
BASS
MEZZO-SOPRANO
SOPRANO
TENOR

INSTRUMENTS
ACCORDION
BANJO
BASS
BONGOS
CELLO
CLARINET
DRUMS
FIDDLE/VIOLIN
FLUTE
FRENCH HORN
GUITAR
HARMONICA
HARP
KEYBOARD
MARACAS
MARIMBA
OBOE
ORGAN
PERCUSSION
PIANO
PICCOLO
RECORDER
SAX
STAND-UP BASS
SYNTHESIZER
TAMBOURINE
TROMBONE
TRUMPET
TUBA
UKULELE

BAND
BIG BAND
BLUES
COUNTRY
ELECTRONIC
HIP-HOP
JAZZ
LATIN

METAL
NEW WAVE
ONE-MAN
POP
PUNK
RAP
REGGAE
ROCK
ROCKABILLY
SWING
WEDDING

COMBAT TRAINING

STAGE COMBAT
DAGGERS
FENCING
HAND-TO-HAND
RAPIER
STAFF
SWORDS

MARTIAL ARTS
AIKIDO
HAPKIDO
JEET JUNE DO
JIU-JITSU
JUDO
KARATE
KUNG FU
TAE KWON DO
TAI CHI
TAIBO

MARTIAL ARTS WEAPONS
BO STAFFS
ESCRIMA
KAMA
NANCHUKAS
SAI
SWORDS
THROWING KNIVES
THROWING STARS
TONFA
MILITARY TRAINING

GENERAL WEAPONS
AUTOMATIC WEAPON
ARCHERY
HANDGUN
RIFLE

IMPROVISATION
GROUNDLINGS
IMPROV (GENERAL)
LONG FORM
SECOND CITY
SHORT FORM
SKETCH
VIOLA SPOLIN

CIRCUS SKILLS
CLOWN
CONTORTIONIST
FIRE EATER
FIRE JUGGLER
HULA HOOP
JUGGLER
MIME
STILT WALKER
TRAPEZE

HORSEBACK RIDING
BARE BACK
BARREL
DRESSAGE
ENGLISH
JUMP
POLO
RODEO
ROPING
SIDE SADDLE
WESTERN

DRIVING SKILLS
4WD
ATV
DUNE BUGGY
MOTORCYCLE, DIRT/ROAD
PRECISION DRIVING
SEMI-TRUCK
STICK SHIFT

MISCELLANEOUS SKILLS
ASTROLOGER
CARPENTRY
CHEF
COMEDIAN
DISC JOCKEY
IMPRESSIONIST
MAGICIAN
MASSEUSE
PILATES
PUPPETRY
SIGN LANGUAGE
STRIPPER
TELEPROMPTER
VENTRILOQUIST
VIDEO GAMES
WHISTLER
YO-YO
YOGA

STUNTS
BMX
BOATING
BUILDING FALL
CYCLING SPILLS
AEROBATIC PILOT
HIGH WIRE
MOUNTAIN BIKING
ROAD DRIVING
SKIING
SKY DIVING
SNOWBOARDING
TRACK DRIVING

THE COVER LETTER

A good cover letter is like a warm handshake. The introductory cover letter should be addressed to a specific person, as is the salutation. If it's "To whom it may concern" or an open-ended "Hi" then it's too impersonal, like a mass mailing. The industry is made up of real people, and you should treat them as such. Look up the agency or casting director in *The Call Sheet*, or another genuine industry publication, and find the name of the specific person of the specific department with whom you want to meet. I promise, if the salutation reads "Dear Agency," your letter will go immediately into the trash.

The body of the cover letter should run 3-4 brief paragraphs, followed by a thank-you. The first paragraph should state the purpose of the letter – who you are, and what you want. The second paragraph talks about your current activity as a working actor. The third paragraph states the contents of the package, "Enclosed is a picture, resume, and demo reel ... " and the last paragraph includes contact numbers, email, and a website URL if available.

The cover letter in an electronic casting submission or email is a bit shorter: Use their name, tell them you're submitting for the role of _____, in the project _____, and that you look forward to meeting them.

DO'S AND DON'TS

1. In the salutation, do address the person either by first name or as Mr. or Ms. coupled with the last name, as in Dear Bobby, or Dear Mr. Wingo. Do not mix the personal first name with the gender title, as in Dear Mr.

Bobby, or Dear Wingo. I've seen this many times – it's a weak start and a red flag that they are dealing with an amateur.

2. Your letter should be light, polite, simple, and brief. Did I mention brief? Do not get cynical, gushy, or philosophical, and don't tell your life story – don't try too hard to sell yourself. Additionally, don't offer emotional baggage, crisis survival stories, or any other personal negative storylines – even seemingly harmless ones like "finally in L.A. after graduating college just to please my parents." You will *not* gain a meeting out of sympathy.

3. Stay away from "student-y" or "I just arrived and am ready to take L.A. by storm!" Instead, provide a professional tone by mentioning your recent or current projects and roles. Your resume will already say everything about your level of experience and status.

4. Do not apologize for your lack of credits. Everyone starts somewhere. In fact, do not apologize for anything. The letter is a handshake, not therapy – be yourself, but be your best self.

5. Make it yours – personality, humor/wit and intent. Be careful with workshops that provide a template – their ideas are very good, but the form is repetitive. Suddenly, casting or rep will get 50 copies of the same letter from actors who took the same workshop. Instead, it should sound like it came from you. Take the ideas offered, but make it yours.

6. Spellcheck everything! Don't distract them with sloppy spelling, grammar, or formatting. Don't blow your first impression and give them an excuse to throw it in the can.

7. If you have a good industry referral, include their name in the opening paragraph. But get their permission ahead of time, because the recipient will probably follow up and call them. You don't want to

blindside your advocate with a cold call. A good industry referral is someone who knows your work, has worked with you in the past, and is in a production position such as a director, casting director, or producer – in other words, someone who has the ability to hire actors. Weak industry referrals include other actors and your high school drama teacher. Another actor can possibly help get your materials to their agent, but it's the people in production who have the most weight.

8. This bears repeating – don't include your home address. Some actors still include a return address on the mailing envelope, but it should *not* be on your photo or resume or cover letter.

9. State your intentions clearly and don't mix your motives – you're either looking for an "audition" from casting or "seeking representation" from an agent or manager. Do not ask an agent to "cast you in something of your type" or ask casting for representation. Some actors reading this will think this is silly, but trust me, I've seen this hundreds of times from amateurs.

10. If submitting to an agency, include qualities you have that the agency might need – you can research that through IMDb Pro or agency books found at bookstores such as Samuel French and Drama Book Shop. Some agency publications have a current list of agency needs at the beginning of the booklet, such as "Looking for Latino males, 25-35" or "Character Actors needed, both genders, 45-75 years and up." Also research online – it's possible that they don't already have someone of your type. Or if your real age is 19-22 but you look 14-17, that's a plus to any agency. There's a high demand for actors like this, because they're able to work longer hours as adults, and the shooting schedule is unhampered by the restrictions of child labor laws.

11. If you already have an agent and are sending an introduction package to a new casting director, use your agency contact information instead of your personal contact information. The only exception to this is when you are submitting yourself for a project that your agent might not, such as an Equity Waiver stage production, or a film if you've only got commercial representation. Some agents will submit theatrically for low-pay/no pay projects while others completely avoid it. So, know your agent's protocol to avoid embarrassing them with a double submission on theatrical projects.

12. After completion, proof for spelling and grammar, and make sure the entire letter is centered on the page. Many actors reveal their inexperience with faulty wording or placing the letter near the top of the page, leaving the second half below blank. It can look sloppy, unbalanced, and unprofessional.

THE PROPER BUSINESS FORMAT OF A LETTER TO A CASTING DIRECTOR, followed by the same to an AGENT/MANAGER is illustrated on the next two pages. Note they are brief, balanced vertically on the page, with left-aligned text. My aside notes are in bold font; do not use them in your own letter. Also, these are bare-bones samples, just to show basic formatting and page layout; they have very little personality. It is up to you to beef it up with your humor and intent. More personable examples of the body of a letter follow these samples.

Date
(3 blank lines)

Name of the Casting Director
Name of Casting Company or Show
Address
City, State, Zip Code
(2-3 blank lines)

Dear Mr. /Ms. _____,
(2 blank lines)

(This is the body of the letter.) I understand that you cast for _____. **(Add a little about what you've been doing lately as an actor.)**

(New paragraph) Please consider me for your next role that calls for someone of my type. If you are open to a Pre-Read, I'd love to come in to meet and read for you.

(New Paragraph) Enclosed please find a photo and resume, and my reel can be seen at ___link___ **(or enclose a disk.)** You can reach me at (888)555-1212, and I look forward to meeting you.
(2-3 blank lines)

Best Regards,
(5 blank lines where you sign your name)

Your name
email
IMDb or website page **(if available)**
(DO NOT ADD YOUR HOME ADDRESS)

Date
(3 blank lines)

Name of the Person
Name of the Agency or Management Company
Address
City, State, Zip Code
(2-3 blank lines)

Dear Mr. /Ms. _____,
(2 blank lines)

(This is the body of the letter.) I'm currently seeking representation. **(Briefly introduce any referrals and describe your current professional activity, relevant background, etc.)**

(New paragraph) Enclosed is a photo, resume and demo reel **(or provide a link to your demo.)** I look forward to meeting and working with you. I can be reached at (888)555-1212.
(2-3 blank lines)

Sincerely,

(5 blank lines where you sign your name)

Your name
email
IMDb or website **(if available)**
(DO NOT ADD YOUR HOME ADDRESS)

SAMPLES OF THE BODY OF THE LETTER:

The following are good examples of the main body of a cover letter that I have found to be personable, witty, and fairly effortless in tone, presentation, and professionalism.

Letter from an actor, fresh out of drama school, in the beginning stages of a career, to a casting director – with a dash of humor in the mix.

Dear Ms. (Last Name),

I understand that you cast for *Grey's Anatomy*. I am currently playing Gertrude in *Hamlet*, and I must say that getting poisoned on a daily basis has really prepared me for playing the victim of a medical emergency.

Please consider me for your next project that calls for someone of my type. If you are open to a pre-read or general, I'd love to come in with a monologue or cold read for you. If you host casting workshops, feel free to add my email to your mailing list.

Enclosed is a photo and resume, and my recent webisode of *Tart* can be viewed at (link.) I can be reached at (phone number.) I look forward to meeting you.

Letter from a fairly established New York actor to a Los Angeles manager, seeking representation. They've been working for about 5 years or more. Additionally, they included a thumbnail of their headshot at the top left of the cover letter, with three strong recent credits next to it in a bold and attractive font.

Hi (Manager's First Name)!

I am seeking management and am in the midst of taking meetings. After hearing such great things about your company from (industry referral), I decided it was time to contact you.

I'm originally from New York and studied at NYU, and since moving here have been through two pilot test deals and some great guest-star roles through my agent, (name of agent) at (agency.) I keep up my skills with improv/sketch comedy at The Groundlings, and am currently in the production of (title of play), as (role), at the (venue name) Theatre.

Enclosed are a few headshots for your review. Feel free to check out my Speedreels demo at (link.) If you'd like to take a meeting, contact me directly at (phone number.)

Thanks so much for your time and consideration. Warmest Regards,

An unconventional, imaginative approach from a mid-level actor, seeking agency representation. The actor description is like that from a dictionary.

Hi (Agent's First Name)!

Johnny McGee [Jah-nee mah-GEE] *Noun:* 1. a wholesome, genuine, but quirky Midwestern athlete. 2. graduate of the University of Texas theatre program. 3. paid-up member of SAG-AFTRA. 4. strong baritone. 5. "Best Actor" at the New York Independent Film Festival. *Verb:* Has booked a slew of independent films in L.A., two web series, national and regional commercials and voice-over gigs.

I am looking for an agent who is just like me: kick-butt and no-holds-barred. I'm a "booker and banker" and together we can move my career forward.

You can check out my reel at (link.) Contact me at (phone number) if you'd like to take a meeting. I look forward to meeting with you.

(Under the signature line, he placed the links to his best episodes in a web series.)

A more conventional letter, but with a highly professional tone from an established talent. They are seeking theatrical representation from an agent and a manager.

Dear _____,

    I just wrapped the film *Crossing Danny*, starring (star name) which is due for release in March. I do well with UTA commercially and am currently taking meetings to find a theatrical agent. *(Substitute "manager" for theatrical agent accordingly)*

    I also recently booked a role opposite (star name) in the upcoming independent film *The Map of Love*, by the same creative team that produced *The Help*, and am scheduled to shoot in Connecticut next month. You can currently see me in a worldwide print and commercial campaign for *DirecTV*, now running nationally.

    I really want to build on this momentum by finding a team of people with the right chemistry. I would love to come by, drop off my demo, and meet with you to see if we're a good fit.

    Thanks!!

Warmest Regards,

Letter from a foreign national with a work Visa, seeking a manager.

Hello _____,

    I'm currently signed with (company name), an aggressive theatrical agency, and am seeking additional management to help strategize the next stage of my career. A quick rundown on my acting is as follows:

    Most recently I guest starred in *Pretty Little Liars* for ABC which was bumped to a recurring role. I also just completed post as voice-over for the feature film *Dead Heat*, starring (star name.) Other recent credits include a guest star on *Castle*, a co-star in the indie film *Only*

My Friends Call Me That, and the lead role in the short film *Lucky Dog.*

I live in Los Angeles fulltime, am a citizen of England and Canada, and am fully capable of working stateside with my Visa. Additionally, I'm fluent in several languages including Persian and French, and quite skilled with New York, Italian, and Russian accents. Included within is a list of several casting directors who know my work and would be happy to provide an endorsement.

My headshot and resume are enclosed for your review. My reel is available online with IMDb. Please contact me at (email) or (phone number) if you'd like to speak further regarding representation.

Best Regards,

These are just a few examples by motivated actors who took the time to put some thought, creativity, and polish into their presentation. Writing a cover letter is time-consuming so make the time. A strong, basic letter can then be altered to personalize each with the name and address of a new recipient.

THE PACKAGE

When seeking representation from an agent or manager, or introducing yourself to a casting director, you will need to send a "package." It should include three things: a photo, a resume, and a cover letter. Include a reel if you have one, or links to performance clips within the letter and on your resume. Mail the package in a crisp manila envelope with a neatly written address. Some industry pros think the hardcopy package is old-school, yet others won't look at you without it. Some state their preference in the agency book. If unstated, send both a hardcopy package and an email with the same material.

WHEN SENDING YOUR PACKAGE AS AN EMAIL to agents and managers for representation it is important that the files are not incompatible or too big. They are busy professionals and anything slow to download gives them an excuse to abort the process and kick you to the curb. Make it easy for them:

1. The cover letter is the body of the email itself.
2. The photo is best sent as a jpeg, at 100dpi resolution, about 200 – 250 kb's.
3. The resume is best sent as an rtf or pdf file, which is compatible to both Mac and PC.

Casting Networks, Actors Access, Now Casting, and Casting Frontier already have your materials in electronic format that are easy to send and easily read. Use the above guidelines, however, when emailing submissions to casting on projects outside these sites.

WHEN SENDING YOUR PACKAGE AS HARDCOPY, always write a brief cover letter explaining why you have sent it. Neglecting this is a weak beginning that I've unfortunately seen a number of times. You may think your objective is obvious, but they can't know what you want if you don't tell them. Always staple the resume to the back of your photo – if it's accidentally separated, they won't know who you are or how to contact you. Trim the resume to the size of your photo.

POINTERS ON TIMING THE MAILOUTS AND PACKAGES:

Sending packages and "ticklers" is a big task and requires that you plan both your time and money. Plan the soft launch to arrive just at or right after the beginning of a season. This means you'll have to back up your preparation date and give yourself plenty of turnaround time to have your photos processed, your postage ready and labels printed, with another day or two for assembly. It's simple, but not easy, and it's all a part of "pounding the pavement."

Pilot season is the busiest time of year – industry professionals are casting both episodics currently on air and pilots (new shows) that they hope will make it on a lineup. Therefore, it's probably the worst time to look for representation. You can try, but if you don't get a response, it's more about the timing than your pitch. Pilots are cast all year, but the meat of the season is still mid-January until mid-April, followed by a six-week hiatus, during which things slow down. Plan to approach representation during slower times just before or after seasons have cycled – they'll have more time to look at your materials with a rested eye. Above all, be patient and consistent and you will eventually get a meeting.

A good way to stay on the radar of a casting office during the heat of any season is to send out what I call "ticklers." These are postcards (4x6, with a postcard stamp, or 5x7 with regular postage.) The postcard features your photo and agency or contact information on the front. If your budget allows, you can print them double-sided with air dates and current activity to show them what you've been doing lately. I normally choose two or three ticklers a year and send these out in cycles – either early pilot season (January); mid-hiatus for the summer films (April/May) and summer theatre auditions (March/April); and/or the fall episodic season (roughly early September or October.)

FINDING REPRESENTATION ONLINE WITH CASTING NETWORKS AND ACTORS ACCESS

If you don't have an agent, Casting Networks hosts "Talent Scout," which adds you to a pool of unrepresented talent and allows agents and managers themselves to search for fresh faces and talent. Actors Access also offers the same opportunity with "Talent Link." I suggest that you do not depend on digital listing alone to find an agent – rather, consider using it as an additional method to bolster your mailouts and packages.

Because it's tricky to find, below are the step-by-step instructions on how to navigate Casting Networks and Actors Access to find the right page and list as an actor seeking representation. The rates will occasionally change for services, so if you are ready for this step, call Casting Networks and Actors Access directly to confirm their prices and locations.

HOW TO LIST AS NON-REPRESENTED TALENT WITH CASTING NETWORKS

Here's the secret deal: "Talent Scout" through Casting Networks is free to their members. That's right, free. And even though Casting Networks weighs in heavily at serving primarily commercial agencies, on Talent Scout you are able choose across the board on the type of representation you're seeking – theatrical, commercial, or management. Here are step-by-step instructions.

1. Log in to your personal account on Casting Networks and click FAQ at the top right of the page menu; another window will open.

2. Near the top left of this page, there's another menu; click "Talent." (No need to sign in again)

3. Click on "Find Representation" in the body of the page, which should land on the "Talent Scout" page. Review their details, and click the blue "Join Now" button.

4. In signing up, check the boxes for the type of representation you seek (Commercial, Theatrical, Modeling, Managers, etc.) Do not check the second box, "not seeking representation," otherwise it will null the above.

Many agents (but not all) are listed with Casting Network's Talent Scout. Casting Networks also hosts your information continuously 24/7.

Los Angeles home page: lacasting.com
San Francisco: sfcasting.com
New York and U.S.: castingnetworks.com

All locations, hours, and contact information:
home.castingnetworks.com/contact

HOW TO LIST AS NON-REPRESENTED TALENT WITH ACTORS ACCESS

To find representation on "Talent Link," you must be registered with an account on Actors Access. Talent Link is $35/month and they automatically send your info to agencies and management companies four times a month. If you list for the 1st of the month, they will automatically repost every week for the full month. If you have a demo reel, they can also download this and attach it as part of your information. To view the page for Talent Link's policies and contact information:

1. Log in to your account and go to the Actors Access homepage.

2. Click on "breakdowns" for Los Angeles. (Or any other city – it's nationwide.)

3. A page listing breakdowns will appear and at the top will be three search boxes.

4. The first one is "search by project title" and the box next to it will be blank. Type "Talent Link" in the blank box.

You'll be directed to the Talent Link posting and page where you can read the policies. You'll see in their policy statements that there is protective screening in place to help you get legitimate requests for a meeting. Not all agents and managers have accounts with Breakdown Services and Actors Access, but most of the legitimate agencies do. To sign up for Talent Link, call Breakdown Services at (310)276-9166 or visit their Cotner office in person.

Actors Access sign-in page: actorsaccess.com
Locations, hours and contact information: actorsaccess.com/content

NOTHING REPLACES THE OLD-SCHOOL HARDCOPY

Not quite yet.

I think the above options provide a wonderful service, and I have known actors who were signed through these digital methods. The selling point on both of these sites is that signing up with these services is cheaper than mailouts. However, I have had many more hits from potential agents on a hardcopy package than on a digital listing. But, if you have the budget, do both. There's also a story near the end of the book entitled "The ABC's of Getting an Agent" that may also give you more insight and the value of my experience.

Above all, be persistent in your hunt for a good agent. Then, be dedicated to becoming a good client.

CHAPTER 3

CASTING AND
AUDITIONS

CASTING DIRECTORS

A casting director has given you an audition. They don't hand out appointments because they think you'll suck, they want you to be good. They're rooting for you to win the role so they can move on to casting the next one. So give up any conspiracy theories and own your powerlessness over decisions actually made by the limits of time, and powers greater than a casting director.

Sure, my personal insecurities have been fooled by the poker face. For months, years, I stood before a casting director, and just when I was sure she hated my guts, she'd book me. That "scowl" was just her face, not me, and certainly not the value my insecurity was giving it. After getting to know her, I discovered what a compassionate and hard-working woman she was. I cannot speak for all casting directors, but I can put myself in their shoes, and it wouldn't be hard to know why their implacable faces are part of the job. They are paid to be neutral third-party observers. Let them do their job. They've read multiple drafts and heard that joke a hundred times – they know it's coming and many times they're even instructed not to laugh. So trust your timing and move the comedy scene forward. They have to scribble notes – it helps them remember you after seeing hundreds of actors, and they may even be writing great things about you. It's their job – let them do their job.

In fact, the dynamics of their livelihood are very similar to ours. They go from show to show, and their next contract is based on how well they cast their last one. They're given very little time to read, prep, and cast a show. Like us, they do the best they can with the time and materials they have. It's not about you. It's not about me. It's not even about them. It's a much bigger picture with a lot more activity and chaos, so when you see that face just remember that it's a raincoat they put on in a storm. Let them have their survival tools. If I were standing in the rain, I'd put one on, too.

Imagine being the middleman for dozens of egos, juggling the budgets and eccentricities of producers, directors, studio execs – not to mention the egos of the crowd of actors they've seen in the last two days. They sometimes witness absurd, aggressive, or cutting personalities, and they absorb all of that on your behalf like a buffer. If they're tough it's because they're good at what they do, and they're just as powerless as we are when the climate changes. Sometimes a major script change comes in seconds before you walk in to read. And the role of the self-deprecating piece of sunshine you were auditioning for has just now been changed into a chain-smoking, ball-busting curmudgeon – using the same scripted dialogue, not a bit of which supports the change. It can be tough on both of you, so be a good sport and weather it together.

The only way to survive the casting cycles is to realize you're not there to book the job – *you're there to make fans*. No canoodling, no BFF's, no ass kissing, just fans. You'll have their respect if you don't fall to pieces because you've let the room rob you of your humanity. All they want to see is actors giving their characters humanity and having an authentic human experience.

So, give casting a break, bring your "A" game, and do your job. The only thing I will ever have power over is preparation and a good attitude. The secret is simple: *Suit up. Show up. Throw down. Go home.*

TYPECASTING

There is a lot of misunderstanding and anxiety regarding typecasting. As actors, we tend to think of ourselves as unique, and we become offended at being put "in a box" because we mistakenly believe that typecasting will reduce us to a cliché. There are also similar words that overlap in meaning and application, including stereotype and archetype. To add to this tangle of "type," advertisers often use archetypes in order to brand, build, and cast their campaigns. Because the terms are so interchangeable in the market (business), it's easy to see why actors (artists) get confused. You can find many online postings and helpful editorials that address this topic and I'm just one more voice. But because it is important to your marketing as an actor, I think it's my obligation to address it from my experience with it in the field.

WHAT IS TYPECASTING?

"Typecasting" actually has a couple of interpretations. For now, let's start with it as a business practice, because it's the first one you'll likely encounter. Typecasting is industry lingo for the process used by casting directors to match actors to the script's description of a character's personality, actions, and physical appearance. Once casting has the production notes, they release them in a "breakdown," and your headshot is submitted for consideration. Casting then finds actors who fit the description in both looks and abilities. So it is a kind of shorthand, and in basic terms it can mean just this: WHAT DO I LOOK LIKE? Now, don't get your knickers in a twist – remember, *it's not personal.* Typecasting is a necessary practice because casting isn't given much lead time to condense the script or start appointments, and they're asked to "lock" the cast by a certain date. This is the most common kind of typecasting you'll experience in the early years of your career. The other kind of typecasting is experienced by established stars who seem to be strongly defined and identified with one particular kind of role – for example, action hero, gritty cop, or sexy spy. Standard breakdowns look something like these:

> LUIS: Latino or African American, MALE, 15 years old (looking for 18 to play younger.) High school athlete, streetwise and hardened by heartbreak. Lives in a broken home with his single mother. Luis' hope and hero, Coach Curtis, is accused of murdering the school principal (after a heated argument over cutting the sports program), then losing his job. GUEST STAR

JOANN: Early to mid-50s, FEMALE. Educated, together, savvy, she has had a tough run, losing a few family members, including her husband to a heart attack. Struggling to stay afloat, she is eager to find closure and move on, but she may have something to hide ... GUEST STAR

ADMINISTRATOR: 45-55, MALE OR FEMALE. The administrator at the Shady Oaks Retirement Community discovers that the kids have been charging the senior residents to read to them and quickly shuts down their operation. Three speeches and four lines, two scenes. CO-STAR. Submit all ethnicities.

BOOM-BOOM: 25-35. Please submit sketch, improv, and comedy actors. Please submit all physical types. This professional clown in full clown regalia parties down at a Halloween bash with his fellow clowns. Comically irascible, he gets into arguments. CO-STAR. PLEASE SUBMIT ALL ETHNICITIES. PLEASE DO NOT COME IN WEARING CLOWN ATTIRE.

You can see that typing has several elements in common: Age, gender, ethnicity, marital status, profession, class distinction/financial status, level of education, traits in humor, personality or even body type, and then a few words about the conflict in the story. At the end there is a contract category that tells the rep the size of the role, which is code for the kind of money you can probably earn on that contract.

Your headshot sends the first message to casting. The actor has a personal appearance and energy that convey an immediate message/impression to the audience. Most actors believe they can play any role, but you need to understand that having range and ability for "What I can do" is not the same as "What do I look like that I can play?" Your headshot spurs the curiosity and imagination of casting toward the possibility, but then your physical presence and talent must fulfill the needs of the character during the audition.

It's crucial that actors develop literacy about their business and realism about their physical look in order to properly shoot marketable headshots, develop talking points with representation, and submit for the proper role. You don't need perfect clarity today, but you should begin now to assess yourself within the market. Clarity and taste will develop over time and with experience.

CATEGORIES IN TYPECASTING

Here's a more detailed breakdown of the categories that agents and casting directors use for typing. You will, in fact, fill out something quite similar to this when you subscribe for an account with the online casting sites.

AGE RANGE

12-18 High School Years
18-24 College Years
22-28 Young Leading Lady/Man
28-35 Young Wife/Mother, Husband/Dad, Professional
32-38 Wife/Husband, Mother/Father, Professional)
35-42 More seasoned, worldly, with earning power
42-48 Same as above, more "character" roles
48-58 Middle-aged character roles, Young
       Grandparents, Judges
58+   Grandparents, Character roles
65+   Elderly, Character roles

GENDER

Male
Female

SEXUAL ORIENTATION

Real-life orientation is not in question here. You should know whether the audience will see/accept you as such, and whether you have the ability to believably play it.

Straight/Heterosexual
Gay/Homosexual
Transgender Identity: Cross Dresser, Transvestite, etc.
Metrosexual: comedic, urban slang for "unknown"
Androgynous

MARITAL STATUS

Do you *look like* you could be single? If so, is it because of youth, or are you an aging bachelor? Are you single by choice or circumstance? Or, do look like you could be married? If so, do you look as if your marriage was old enough to produce kids, or is it still too soon for that? Or, do your eyes and face have the experience to say that "divorced," even "widowed," is possible?

ETHNIC APPEARANCE AND NATIONALITY

Ethnic appearance and nationality are perfect examples to illustrate that it doesn't matter what you are, it's what you LOOK like you might be. Make no mistake, this is an asset, especially to your resume, when you have the dialects or languages to back that up. Films in the spy, fantasy, war, and martial arts genres are routinely hiring characters with foreign loyalties. And the 'search du jour' in commercial and theatrical markets is for the "ethnically ambiguous." Cast a wide net and you'll always be working.

APPEARANCE	NATIONALITY
African American	American
Asian	Australian
Caucasian	British
East Indian	Cuban
European	French
Hispanic	German
Middle Eastern	Hawaiian
Native American	Kenyan
Pacific Islander	Irish
Scandinavian	Italian

CASTING CATEGORIES

Some casting sites and publications divide men and women into two categories: Leading Man/Lady (includes young leading man/lady and supporting leads) and Character/Comedian. You list yourself in either category and within your age group. You are also able to list yourself as a combo, like Leading Lady/Character Actress.

Leading categories often require a physical beauty, chemistry, and the stamina of a champ to carry a show as the "name above the title." Yet physical beauty will not be enough – these roles also require training, taste, intelligence, a fine voice, and a certain nobility of the soul.

Character categories are traditionally cast according to quirkier and offbeat looks with more eccentric qualities in height, weight, build, and voice. In the past, they were relegated to either supporting leads or smaller featured parts. In contemporary times, however, the definition of "character" has been widened to embrace behavior and psychology. Character actors can now be leads (Steve Buscemi, John C. Reilly, Jack Black, Michael Cera), and leading actors are now embraced in character parts (George Clooney, Cate Blanchett, Daniel Day Lewis, Charlize Theron, and Meryl Streep.)

Comedians of both genders can be either leading or character in look, but comedy demands a finely tuned sense of humor in timing, physical agility, and wit. It's possible for an actor to play different types of humor, but when pitching yourself to an agent, you should know which of these is closest to your own personality, and where this matches a current film or TV show.

KNOW YOUR HUMOR:

Know the seat of your natural humor, the one that you do the best. Humor is needed for both comedy and drama. Comedy is not just the set-up and punch line for a sitcom or broad farce, and many believe that at the heart of every joke is the seed of tragedy. "Humor is the mistress of tears." – William Makepeace Thackeray. So consider this when working on a dramatic role, too. The finest villains are played well by actors who understand black humor (e.g. Alan Rickman, John C. Reilly, and Don Cheadle.) The blessing of knowing how to play all styles of comedy is embodied in the work of Sandra Bullock (*While You Were Sleeping, Miss Congeniality, The Proposal* and *The Blind Side*.) So if you tell an agent "I'm funny" it doesn't mean anything. Which one of these fits you best? Are you:

- Made for madcap farce and broad, physical comedy? Can you handle a zany slapstick or pratfall? Or, are you

- A member of the "Ironic Class?" Do you underplay with subtle sarcasm and a wry smile? Can you mix in a little starch with that taunt?

- How about soft boxing with some classy banter? Are you armed with clever wit and a snappy comeback? Amusing, cheeky, with just the right balance of recreational wordplay?

- Are you salty and irreverent? Grounded and earthy with an appreciation for a lusty innuendo, even vulgar profanity?

- Or are you charming and cheerful with an infectious giggle? All whimsy and bubbles with a goofy, childlike enthusiasm?

- Then there's the open simplicity and sincerity of stating your "beliefs", no matter how ridiculous, unfounded or illogical. The contemporary malapropism requires an innocent faithfulness, often used in mockumentaries and satire. It's the 'dumb blonde' of Realism.

Look at the current listings of films released and television programming - which movies or shows incorporate the above? Never mind what you enjoy watching, it's what you do well that counts. Every style of humor has its own rhythm and demands, and there is great joy and satisfaction in playing them well. Make sure you are equipped and ready when the script calls for them.

CLASS DISTINCTION

The types of roles you're submitted for will also depend on the class, level of education, and profession that you're able to project. Again, it's not what you are, it's what you look like. I've known actors who came from terrible poverty whose cheekbones and spirit said "nobility."

American Class Structure:	**European Class Structure:**
Wealthy (trust fund baby)	Royalty and aristocracy
Upper class (white-collar)	Middle class (merchant, trade)
Middle class (suburban)	Peasants (farmers, laborers)
Lower middle class, blue-collar	Clergy
Poverty (street level)	Military

EDUCATION

Ask yourself honestly: Do you immediately project the energy of a high school graduate or a dropout? Two years of college? College grad? With just a Bachelor's degree, or an MBA or PhD? Legal or medical school?

PROFESSIONS

What does your appearance say about the job you might hold? Consider your age and your class distinction, then get more specific. For example, a bartender in a college blues bar is a different look than a bartender in a five-star hotel or a bartender in Hell's Kitchen. Or a teacher – kindergarten or college professor? Military – senior officer, or bootcamp? Many actors generalize their type, "I'm a cop." Look, get specific, a cop is not just some guy with a badge and a gun – do you look like a seasoned detective or a rookie patrolman?

PERSONALITY TYPES

Personality types are also referred to as "character elements," "essence," or "states of being" and are not as easily defined as emotions. They require thoughtful and conscientious development when the script calls for them, especially if they're outside your natural seat. Here are a few examples:

Obsessive/Compulsive	Quiet/Introspective	Gregarious/Carefree
Sexy/Sensual/"Player"	Intellectual	Temperamental/Moody
Sporty/Athletic	Tough/Gritty	Eccentric/Quirky
Earthy/Warm	Cold/Calculating	Friendly/Outgoing
Responsible	Flaky	Phony
Competitive	Peaceful	Lazy
Worrier/Uptight	Loyal	Bitter/Suspicious
Generous	Stingy	Depraved/Lewd
Addictive	Plans/Organized	Impulsive
Innocent/Virginal	Holy/Pious	Curious
Dangerous	Stubborn	Adorable/Charming
Mischievous	Rebellious	Jaded/Cynical

List your own personality traits. Make another list of traits you think you can move closer to with more practice, then find relevant scenes to work on in an acting class.

GENRES OF PLAYS AND SCREENPLAYS

Each of these has a specific style and form that the actor must shape himself to fit – either in physical presence, vocal energy and attack, or in psychological and emotional response.

Romance	Family Films
Romantic Comedy	Comedy (dry to madcap)
Road/Buddy	Animated
Thriller/Suspense/Mystery	Documentary/Mockumentary
Action/Adventure	Westerns
Horror	Wartime/Military
Science Fiction/Fantasy	Crime/Gangster
Epic/Historical	Musicals
Sports	Martial Arts
Film Noir	

Now, let's clear up some of the differences between typecasting, stereotypes, and archetypes.

STEREOTYPE

"In your choices lies your talent." – Stella Adler

Remember that typecasting is a necessary business practice that serves a production schedule and a budget; it's not the interpretation and execution of the role itself. That's the actor's job. In my experience, a stereotype (also known as a cliché), is different than typecasting, and I consider it the actor trap. The actor trap is when you play "Type" as a "Stereotype" and boil a character down to the lowest common denominator with weak and predictable choices. If the frightened actor chooses to be "safe" and only "give them what he thinks they want," he may lose depth, novelty, and humanity. I believe mediocrity is criminal – I'd rather be awful and learn something, than be just average and unmemorable. Review your choices for behavior, activity, personality/essence, and dressing for the part, then ask yourself: Have I copied something or someone? Is it flat and two-dimensional? Am I playing of the "idea" of the character, the "outside" of this character?

You need to have your own original moments within the logic of the script. Be sure to work deeper, not bigger, and go for the inside of the character.

A good example of "type" that is easily clichéd is that of the hooker, the trashy stripper, or the gangster's moll. Shallow interpretation of this is to play the "idea" of her, from the outside. Predictable clichés range from gum-smacking "knockers up" and platinum hair, to a soft porn fly girl someone saw pushing sexy in a music video.

My favorite actresses to play this type are Shirley MacLaine (*Sweet Charity, Irma la Douce, The Apartment, Some Came Running*), Lesley Ann Warren (*Victor Victoria*), Mira Sorvino (*Mighty Aphrodite*), and Charlize Theron (*Monster.*) Great actors never take their beauty and skill for granted. They are always pushing the edge, challenging the form, moving the cliché to the iconic.

Stereotypes and clichés are in some ways watered-down versions of Commedia Dell'Arte, which has stock characters. Stock characters have been around for hundreds of years. They have a place and a purpose, but they can't always do justice to complicated social conflicts, a deviant psyche, or the entangled heart of some contemporary scripts.

You always have the choice to breathe fresh life into old forms, but you have to understand the form first. It's important that you make informed choices.

Instead of pulling a role down and playing it from the outside, try lifting yourself up to the inner size and scope of the character. Studying archetypes is a good place to start.

ARCHETYPE

Archetypes are different from typecasting and stereotype/cliché in that they're eternal, noble, and highly developed. They do not exist just for the sake of outward appearance or lack of time. Archetypes have been used extensively by writers, directors, and storytellers throughout the ages and across many cultures. As anchors in storytelling, they bring a largeness of form and truth. They are muses, ideas, and ideals; they exemplify profound human interaction and struggles that have existed throughout time. The story presents them as individuals, but they actually represent the thousands of men and women like them. Archetypes are universal teachers, they inspire the listener and challenge the audience to see themselves and each other more clearly. They are especially important for actors playing leads and supporting leads to understand when breaking down scripts and building a character. Use of them can ground you with inspiration, power, and surprise.

Every story has a hero. Every hero hosts an archetype, and is surrounded by characters in the story who are archetypes as well. Carl Jung, Joseph Campbell, Dr. Carol Pearson and others have written extensively about this. Each archetype has essential qualities and challenges they overcome, and their choices are colored by either the dark or virtuous side of their psyche, depending upon their stage of the journey. I have personally used all these resources and have them in my library of acting resources. I strongly recommend you do, too. For example, here are the archetypes presented by Dr. Pearson: The Innocent, the Orphan, the Warrior, the Caregiver, the Seeker, the Destroyer, the Lover, the Creator, the Ruler, the Magician, the Sage, and the Fool. Her descriptions are beautifully written and explored in *The Hero Within,* and *Awakening the Heroes Within.* These resources allow me look at a script differently, and can add dimension and texture to a role.

Many respected actors have built successful careers because they had the ability to combine several basic archetypes, which increased their range and extended their earning power. You can have, literally, hundreds of choices: regular guy + hero, fool + creator, innocent + seeker, and lover + sage. Examples: Cate Blanchett (*Elizabeth,* and as Bob Dylan in *I'm Not There*), Ben Kingsley (*Gandhi, Sexy Beast, Schindler's List*), Ed Norton (*American History X , The Score, Fight Club*), Phillip Seymour Hoffman (*Flawless, Capote*) and of course Meryl Streep, Daniel Day Lewis, Mark Strong, Robert Downey, Jr., and Johnny Depp.

Actors must bring surprise and innovation to the audition for which they've been typecast. Bruce Willis has portrayed a number of cops (for example, the *Die*

Hard franchise, and *16 Blocks*), but he lifted himself up to the size of the archetype, and turned in memorable interpretations of the *man* in that profession. He wasn't a "type", "just a cop," he played each differently with a specific point of view and life experience. With depth, duty, and understanding, you too can create surprising combinations of your abilities in archetypal roles. But first things first, let's get on a path that lets you do this well!

WORK SMARTER, NOT HARDER

Work through your agent.

The above is the best overview and clarification I can give you of the "typing" process that most casting and agents use when they assess your look. You're not obliged to be passive. Your own vision and abilities are the keys to enlarging and refining any generalizations. Be realistic with yourself. If you are limited in range, then accept it, but *be great at it.* If you have mad skills, then go for it, but don't claim versatility unless you can back it up with excellent skills. A greater range can help your agent cast a wider net and pitch hard for you when the casting office is dubious. You can bolster the agent's confidence by working on a risky role in a stage play or by having them ask casting for a pre-read if they "don't see you that way."

You can also develop talking points with reps by asking yourself: Which high-profile actors, films or shows currently on the air match your look, sensibility, or style of delivery? Knowing this "hook" can be helpful in meetings to find rep, or in career development once you're signed. For example, you may be 20, but you look 16, which means there's a bigger market for you in teenaged projects. You might also consider the weight of experience your eyes reflect. You may be 20, but your eyes say 40, so you might play older, not just your age range. Address and correct any misconceptions, too, that might "type you out" incorrectly. Recently one of my students completely stunned me. The name on the roster was Japanese, but in walked a freckled All-American redhead – his mother was Scottish. Because of his name, however, he'd be automatically pulled for Asian roles, yet his look simply does not support it. To submit for Caucasian roles, he is considering a new stage name as a fix.

In the beginning stages of your career, just start with what's offered. Start with where you are. Develop a relationship and good communication with your agent so you'll have the freedom and trust to let them help you. For casting, it is essential that you do some homework before your meeting to find out about their shows. Know the show, know your type, know your market, and bring in the goods that accentuate your strengths. Very often, the final say on your type will be with the casting director – not you and not your agent. Above all, just stay ready and flexible. In the beginning, I could get seen only for the All-American upper middle-class sweetie with a twist of sexy. With faithful and persistent diligence, my agent was able to get me seen for self-deprecating nuns, feisty biker chicks, the peevish nurse, the heartless mother, and the grifting vixen.

REVEALING YOUR TYPE IN HEADSHOTS

If you are represented, ask them how they see you and what they need for submissions. Sometimes a good photographer will provide insight, other times you're on your own to make the decisions. Appearance (clothes, hairstyle, and physical condition) will say a lot about your type. *Make distinctive, simple and crisp choices that are versatile across different genres.* If you are seen more as a well-groomed, slick CEO type, then make sure you get that suit shot and look sharp. If you are obviously a beefy construction worker, don't put on a thousand-dollar suit and try to sell corporate. If you're a slender brainiac, don't wear plaid and try to sell concrete. Find your natural space, and be the best, not "the rest." Now for those of you who are saying "duh, who doesn't know this?" I say to you, I've seen it. I've seen the older gents in toupées hoping to capture the romantic leads of the younger set. It's not pretty.

Blank eyes on a pretty face is not interesting. The most interesting shots are when the eyes convey specific thoughts and messages, but the message has to be in balance with the messenger. Your insides need to match your outsides, so carefully consider your inner dialogue during the shoot. Many newcomers self-sabotage by attempting to be all things to all people all at once. They cram the wrong character into a look, which short-circuits the effect and diminishes its versatility to reach a lot of shows. One young actor I saw was a sun-kissed and fun innocent dressed very colorfully and attractively in cool skateboarding clothes. He was an obvious shoo-in for the romantic lead, funny sidekick, teen adventure, and national commercial – but his eyes had the bloodlust of a violent nightmare, a killer. This shot was right only for a one-time role in a slasher film. It was a huge disconnect and he couldn't understand why agents and casting wouldn't bite at his picture. If this is you, reshoot and discipline your inner dialogue to elevate, not decapitate, the look. If you want to promote yourself as edgy, then it's appropriate to flirt with dark and dangerous, or "open with a twist"– but wear the proper clothing that will support that image.

THE UGLY SIDE OF TYPECASTING

Later in your career, it is especially important that you recognize when you've been "typed out" – once a cop, always a cop. It can be a tough spot no matter where you are on the ladder of success, but many enjoy very long careers because of it. It all depends on how you choose to view it. Some casting directors see me only as comedic, while others know my dramatic chops. Some are convinced I'm a middle class beauty queen or upscale trophy wife, but others love to bring me in for the low-brow character twists. I know who I am, it's not my job to convince an unwilling eye to see otherwise. It's my job to seek out the willing and then show up and throw down. The body of work will speak for itself. The brilliant and wonderful Melissa McCarthy never settles for just her physical type as a "traditional stock character" – she is without question a leading lady and continues to surprise, confound, and astonish us with her mighty, mighty talent and beautiful charisma.

So, pick your battles. If you're blonde and they're looking for a redhead, they'll cast a redhead. If you're 5'9" but the leading man is 5'7", they'll go shorter. Learn to let go of the things you can't change. It's enough that your talent got you in the room, gave them options, and the other actors a run for their money. Typecasting is a necessary process, not a necessary evil. It can turn against you only if you let it. You can make typecasting beneficial if you use it to clarify a starting point for your career, and as a base of discussion with an agent or manager. Enlarge it through training then, make it work for you by taking risks in new areas. Typecasting is only a temporary obstacle and, as in life, all obstacles should be seen as just that: temporary. Stay open and flexible, and remember: *It's not personal.*

CHOOSING AUDITION MATERIAL – STAGE, TV AND FILM

ARM YOUR ARSENAL

A variety of monologues and scenes are essential tools in the actor's toolbox. In my book, they're not just tools, they're weapons – weapons of beauty, of destruction, of the sacred and the meek. All actors should have an arsenal of good scenes and monologues ready at any time for any occasion. I can think of a dozen life-defining moments in my early years when I was thrown into sudden situations, used my monologues, and furthered my career. Luck was nothing more than preparation meeting opportunity.

CHOOSING MATERIAL FOR TV/FILM

CASTING DIRECTORS AND TALENT REPS

A meeting (not an audition) with a TV/Film casting director for the first time is called a "general." Generals in the old-school sense are a thing of the past, but they are still done at the special request of an agent, manager, network, or studio in order to meet new faces and talent. In generals with casting, and in meetings with potential agents and managers, it's often a mixture of a "getting to know you" interview and a conversation, plus a prepared monologue or scene.

Some casting directors will not want a prepared monologue, but may instead ask you to cold-read sides from the show just to see how you handle their material. Not every office runs its meetings the same way, but here are some suggestions and guidelines based on common experiences across the board.

If you need to find audition monologues for Los Angeles industry generals and meetings, find two contrasting monologues of only 45 seconds to one minute each in length – one dramatic and one comedic. Unlike theatre, any medium is appropriate – stage, television, film, or literary cuttings delivered with energy appropriate for camera. Anything you choose should have been published and/or produced projects, *not* something you wrote yourself.

For casting directors, <u>find something close to the style and genre of their current shows; this can be especially useful when needing material for a workshop they're moderating</u>. A common mistake is choosing a dark or graphic monologue to impress the casting director with dramatic skills, completely disregarding the fact that the director casts for a fun physical comedy. If casting asks you to cold-read a scene from one of their projects, it doesn't mean you're actually auditioning for that part; they just want to see how you handle the style and rhythm of their show. They'll allow you time to prepare, anywhere from 5 to 20 minutes outside in the hallway, so cold readings are not actually "cold." Remember, you're there to act, not read.

With an agent or manager meeting, you should follow the same guidelines, except you do not have to shape it toward a particular show. But do find something appropriate to your type. If you don't know your type, just do something in your age range and gender, and something that you love, love, love to say. Desire is all.

Sometimes a rep will ask you to bring in a scene instead of a monologue. Choose an acting partner who is equally talented, one who is willing to give you the meat of the dialogue and focus, and who's self-disciplined enough to not upstage you.

I know you've all heard the stories about the agent signing your partner instead of you, but choosing a weak acting partner to avoid this dilemma will *not* make you look better. Instead, a less-than-great partner irritates and distracts the agent from focusing on you. Direct it realistically and subtly to make yourself the point of focus while maintaining chemistry with your partner. The worst scenes to watch are those with talking heads in profile.

For both casting and reps, *"lead with your strong suit."* This means, do what you do best and what you're cast-able in today.

Many will watch only the first monologue and see your potential in the first 20 seconds. They may not ask to see the second one, but you should have it prepared in case they say, "Nice, but I don't really see you playing that; or, it's not right for our show. Have anything else?" Choose your second scene or monologue for contrast in character and tone.

CHOOSING MATERIAL: SHOWCASES AND WORKSHOPS

Although I don't personally choose to attend these, another way actors meet casting directors (and agents) is to sign up for a showcase or workshop. Most will ask for the same as discussed above, but specify limits on the time, pages, or the number of pieces you can perform.

Pay attention to the fine print on the workshop websites. Each moderator (casting director or agent) will have personalized, detailed instructions on what they want the actors to bring; and very often they'll ask that you may only use the pre-approved listing of material that is already in the host's database. Every session moderator is different. One says it's okay to use Shakespeare, another brings in their own cold readings, another says bring your own monologue, and the next one will see only scenes. The face-to-face also changes accordingly as well. One moderator only gives group Q&A with no face time, while another gives written comments on a card regarding your read, and yet others grant 5 minute, private, one-on-one chats. It just depends upon the individual who's moderating that particular session.

Follow the guidelines posted, and if you're able to bring in your own material, choose something close to the style and genre of the Casting Director's show. Don't wait until the last minute to learn new material – it needs time to ripen, and that in itself will give you confidence.[2]

CHOOSING AUDITION MATERIAL FOR THEATRE

Although most actors in Los Angeles are pursuing careers in film or television, many are well trained in theatre. Much of that opportunity is unfortunately unpaid in the Equity Waiver scene, but there is still plenty of opportunity to audition in L.A. for paid work at local Equity theatres, regional theatres, and even New York casting calls. The theatre community has its own protocol and integrity for auditions; you should respect it by preparing fully and carefully.

Most theatres require two contrasting monologues from published plays, mixing comedic/dramatic with contemporary/classical, and usually with a combined total time limit of three (up to five) minutes. Review the specific requests of each theatre, as some may have slight variations regarding time limits. If you go over their time specs, you will be cut off before you finish.

---

[2] *Please visit the chapter on "Scams: Workshops, Showcases and Online Webinars" for links to find legitimate, licensed workshops.*

So, for an audition asking for a total of three minutes, I'd suggest a time of 1:15 minutes to 1:45 minutes maximum for either monologue in order to comply with the time limit.

Again, use only published playwrights – using television or film material is offensive to theatre people. Focus on what you can be cast in today, within your own age range and abilities, and don't overreach for roles outside of that. I can assure you they will not hire a 25-year-old for King Lear, or a 40-year-old for Romeo. (Don't laugh, I've seen this more than I care to remember.)

For stage, using your own material, song lyrics, or monologues that aren't from a published play is an indication that you're green – an amateur. The other red flag of the amateur is presenting the material without having first read the play. In TV and film, actors are used to not reading a full script beforehand because it's usually not available. However, most plays are usually accessible, and you must make every effort to read it. Theatre auditors are quite literate, and they'll know instantly if the actor is not familiar with the play and the author's intent. I strongly urge you to read the entire play to inform your choices when rehearsing, and that you completely immerse yourself in the material daily, with hours of work. If you go in under-rehearsed for a stage audition, the shot of adrenalin overpowers your prep, and the sad result is overacting, "freezing up" and dropping lines.

Before making your final selection for Leagues, for instance, look at the theatre's upcoming season and consider choosing material related to their authors and plays. But unless it's specifically requested, do not audition with a Hamlet monologue if they're mounting *Hamlet,* or Blanche if they're mounting *A Streetcar Named*

Desire. Instead, choose another Williams play, or a Shakespeare character with a similar temperament.

In Chapter 5, "Auditions for Theatre," is the *URTA NUIA Handbook (for Actors).* This comprehensive manual not only has the do's and don'ts of choosing material, it also suggests appropriate staging and insightful delivery techniques to help you do your best work. You can find more information on URTA and choosing material for stage online at urta.com.

One of the sad, common actor traps is to wait until the last minute, then grab for something mediocre, even if the material doesn't really speak to you. You know in your gut that the character is just "meh, okay," and guess what? That's what they're saying about your performance, too.

Stella Adler used to say *"If you're bored, you're boring."* Desire is everything. If you love your material, chances are they will as well. So don't wait, start now to arm your arsenal. Above all, no matter what form or medium you pursue, remember you're an actor, and your heart should beat as a character who is a flesh-and-blood human being, not an actor playing a part. Focus all your energy on the task at hand: choose strong and beautiful material that will allow you to create a lasting and memorable experience – for yourself and for them.

SUGGESTED RESOURCES IN PRINT AND ONLINE

ONLINE SITES FOR AUDITION MATERIAL:
(Free downloads for Stage, Television and Film)

Drew's Script-o-Rama: script-o-rama.com
Simply Scripts: simplyscripts.com

Theatre on a Shoestring:
upstagereview.org/linksmonologues.html
Project Gutenberg (free ebooks and plays): www.gutenberg.org
Monologue Archive: monologuearchive.com
Colin's Movie Monologue Page: whysanity.net/monos
Actor Point: actorpoint.com/monologue.html
Shakespeare Monologues: shakespeare-monologues.org
Library of Congress Federal Theatre Project Collection, 1935-1939: http://lcweb2.loc.gov/ammem/fedtp/fthome.html
These Aren't My Shoes: notmyshoes.net/monologues/
Arts on the Move:
artsonthemove.co.uk/resources/scripts/scripts.php

EXAMPLES FROM LITERATURE:

Charles Bukowski, *Burning in Water, Drowning in Flame*
Walt Whitman, *Leaves of Grass*
Albert Camus, *The Stranger; The Fall*
Alexander Pushkin, *Eugene Onegin; The Prisoner of the Caucasus*
William Ernest Henley, *Invictus*
John Steinbeck, *East of Eden* (the novel, not the screenplay)
Fyodor Dostoyevsky, *The Brothers Karamazov*

MONOLOGUE BOOKS IN PRINT

For the purpose of this section, I'm rather partial to a few monologue books for timed auditions and fresh material:

222 Monologues, 2 Minutes and Under series, various Editors, published by Smith and Kraus.

The Methuen Book of ... series, various Editors, published by Methuen Publishing Ltd., excellent taste in classical material (and contemporary fare).

Ten-Minute Plays from the Actors Theatre of Louisville, various Editors, published annually by Samuel French.

The Ultimate Scene and Monologue Sourcebook by Ed Hooks, published by Back Stage Books, 2007. Cross-reference material according to gender, age, and story synopsis.

CHAPTER 4

TV AND FILM

AUDITIONS

GETTING STARTED ONLINE: SUBMISSIONS AND CASTING

Gone are the days of the agency submission with a hardcopy photo and resume. Many, if not most, submissions to stage, television, film, and commercials are now done electronically. Casting directors, agents, and managers use primarily four sites: Breakdown Services' Actors Access, Casting Networks, Casting Frontier, and NOW Casting. NOTE: breakdowns are free to view at each of these sites. To submit, however, you will need an account (free) and payment arrangements for the job submission(s.) The cost is reasonable.

If you're planning an acting career, with or without representation, setting up accounts with these websites is important. Their function and services are similar; their differences are subtle. My theatrical agents (stage, TV and film) are with Breakdown Services/Breakdown Express, so I use Actors Access for theatrical projects. My commercial agents are with Casting Networks and Casting Frontier, so I field my commercial auditions through them. Breakdown Services tends to host most of the film, television, and stage projects but also many commercial projects. Casting Networks is the reverse – it weighs in heavily with commercial breakdowns and then theatrical projects. But both companies offer up-to-date breakdowns on projects across all media, both union and non-union. Every casting director and representative in Los Angeles, New York, and the major regional markets use these companies, and they're considered the legitimate source for casting and actor submissions.

The other legitimate sites with similar services are NOW Casting, Casting Frontier, and Backstage. I consider all these sites necessary and useful, but you must choose for yourself according to your budget, career path and your agent's preference. You simply must join the digital age if you want to survive in the industry. *NOTE: rates occasionally change for services, sometimes without notice. So when you are ready for this step, check to confirm prices and locations.*

BREAKDOWN SERVICES™ and ACTORS ACCESS™

Breakdown Services: breakdownservices.com
Actors Access: actorsaccess.com
For locations, hours, and contact information:
actorsaccess.com/content

Breakdown Services hosts a full spectrum of services to all members of the industry, and each service supports the other. For instance, Breakdown Express is the part of Breakdown Services dedicated to casting directors and talent representatives to post and make submissions. *Actors Access is the actor part of Breakdown Services.* For the newcomer, the process is this: casting posts a breakdown, the agent submits your profile for a role, you're emailed an appointment, and then you download your sides through Showfax – all this is available from one site, Breakdown Services. This path and process are what all of the listing sites share and have in common.

So to clarify, Actors Access is the actor part of Breakdown Services. Once the actor registers, their profile (resume, pictures, demo reels) is available electronically to use for submissions. Unrepresented actors can still self-submit to projects posted on breakdowns, too.

Actors Access is free to join and anyone can check out the breakdowns at no charge. However, if you want to submit yourself for a project, you'll need to set up an account, and registration is simple. Get a username and password, upload your photo (the first two are free) and type in your resume. Afterward, you can self-submit to any of the projects listed. There is a $2 charge per submission. However, with a $68 yearly subscription to Showfax, you get unlimited submissions and sides to download at no additional cost.

Although Actors Access is free, the other services at Breakdown Services have separate fees. These include Casting and Agency labels, Talent Link (to find an agent online), Media Bank (to post your demo reel), Eco-Cast (for electronic auditions, shot at the Cotner home base or Argentum Casting Suite), and Casting About (to find casting offices.) For more information, visit Breakdown Services and Actors Access online.

CASTING NETWORKS

Los Angeles home page: lacasting.com
San Francisco: sfcasting.com
New York/National: castingnetworks.com
Hours, location and contact:
castingnetworksinc.com/contact
FAQ page: home.lacasting.com/helpfaq/faq

Casting Networks is similar to Breakdown Services' Actors Access, but is used primarily by commercial casting and agents for electronic listings and submissions. Their breakdowns also include film and television. If you have an account, resources include media hosting for your demo reel; agency, manager, and casting directories and free labels. Register first and you'll be issued a username and password.

OF NOTE: There is no charge if your agency already has an account to service their client roster. If you are repped, but the agency doesn't have an account, the $25 set-up fee is waived. If not repped, the set-up fee is added. There are three payment plan options:

1. Prepay 1 Year, get 2 months free. Total cost is $174.50 (includes a $25 fee-up fee and discount.) This plan includes unlimited submissions and media hosting. $14.95/month thereafter.

2. Prepay 6 Months and get one month free. Total cost is $99.75 (includes $25 set-up fee and discount.) Then, $14.95/month thereafter.

3. Month to Month: $25 set-up fee + $14.95/month thereafter.

Free unlimited submissions, media hosting, and Talent Scout can be included in all three plans. If you are self-submitting without an agent, or signed with an agency but want to self-submit for projects outside their interest (e.g. low-budget films, or another medium they don't cover), submissions are $1.49 each.

Casting Networks offers even more options and price points. Check their FAQ page or call them for more information.

CASTING FRONTIER

castingfrontier.com

Casting Frontier is another full-service casting site similar to the others, but it offers its own brand of additional features. If you are planning a career in commercials, being a part of both Casting Networks and Casting Frontier is probably in your best interest. Setting up your profile is the same as with the other companies. Additional details can be found online at castingfrontier.com/talent.

1. Basic Profile – Free. Includes one headshot, a resume, one ID, unlimited changes.

2. Premium Profile – $10/month or $60/year

3. Premium Profile Plus – $15/month or $80/year

Unlike any of the others, Casting Frontier assigns a bar code, called a Talent ID number, to each actor. It's scanned at the audition, replacing the traditional sign-in, and it automatically downloads your profile for the session. You can purchase a card for your wallet, print one out from home as needed, or add it to your hardcopy resumes as a permanent feature. Additional services at Casting Frontier include receiving daily and direct emails of the casting calls, real-time audition posting, editing, and production playback as well as free apps for iPads, iPhones, or Androids.

NOW CASTING

nowcasting.com
Location, hours, and contact information:
nowcasting.com/contactus.php

NOW Casting has very similar features, but unique benefits, and considered budget-friendly. If you are a new actor to the L.A. market, NOW Casting can be a great place to start, and many of my peers are with them. One difference between NOW Casting and the others is even though they aren't widely utilized by agents and managers, some very big casting rooms, studios, and executives (such as Tyler Perry, SONY, ABC, and Lionsgate to name a few) are loyal clients and hire through NOW Casting. They still receive the same up-to-date casting notices, which means you still have access and can submit to Union projects. They also offer free sides to Union Actors, or Actors represented by Union franchised agencies, agencies under ATA/NATR, and some qualified Managers. Here are their packages and additional perks:

1. FREE registration; with 6 free photos at any one time (other sites limit the number of photos); free uploads for photos; searchable by Casting Directors, Agents and Managers.
2. Reels and Clips: $6.00/month
3. The Professional: $11.00/month
4. The Professional Plus: $16.00/month
5. The Works: $21.00/month
6. The Promoter: $13.00/month

Now Casting is very competitive in providing actors with full professional tools to develop their careers by offering Auditions NOW (to electronically submit your self-taped audition), Contacts NOW (comprehensive database of projects currently casting, including addresses), Postcards NOW (to design, label and mail from your computer), and Websites NOW. Now Casting can be vital to the working actor engineering the early stages of their career by providing good information, reasonable costs and professional services, especially to those who are not represented or signed to an agent in only one medium.

BACKSTAGE.COM (Online version of *Backstage Magazine* and *The Call Sheet* publications)

Backstage.com also hosts additional opportunities to find auditions nationwide. It is updated daily, and is another option for an actor's electronic profile. *Backstage Magazine* has historically been the go-to trade magazine and resource center for actors, successfully bridging the east and west coasts. Companies like this have the confidence of the acting community. Go online to backstage.com and backstage.com/subscribe to find casting notices, casting directors, and agents in your area, and to backstage.com/subscribe to start your account. Even if you don't have an account, one beautiful perk free for all actors is the *Backstage Message Board* – a dedicated support forum for actors to talk to each other regarding all things show biz – from craft to commerce. *Back Stage Espresso* can also email daily with well-produced newsletters highlighting current projects in all mediums, for both coasts and the regional markets. I also highly recommend their *The Call Sheet*, a smaller paperback with full listings of casting directors, talent agents and managers, films and television production, and a listing of unions and guilds. It is updated frequently and covers both coasts.

THE TRUTH ABOUT BREAKDOWNS if you don't have an agent or manager is that not all breakdowns are posted for actors to see and self-submit. The big shows and casting houses simply will not list for every episode or consider an actor without an agency referral. But there are plenty of other paying projects available for you to submit.

Whether you're union or non-union, represented or not represented, these services enable you to be pro-active in booking your own work and building your resume. You simply have to self-submit if you're not signed to a rep, and you can still use these services even if you're not "signed across the board." For instance, if you're signed to a commercial agent, that agent will submit you for commercial projects (and you won't), but you can still submit yourself to stage, television, and film breakdowns and fill that void. Occasionally, casting still goes old-school and requests hardcopies of your photo and resume by messenger, but the current casting practice is now almost overwhelmingly by electronic submissions, and they use these companies: Breakdown Services, Casting Networks, Now Casting, Casting Frontier, and Backstage.

THE NUTS AND BOLTS

THE TECHNICAL SIDE OF THE AUDITION ROOM

1. Prep your script: Highlight or mark your lines on the page. This will make them easier to find as you're using the page.

2. Review the sides and carefully consider as many of the circumstances as time permits. Circumstances are the who, what, where, when, how and why of the scene. Depth of understanding is far better than rote memorization painted over with an emotional wash. The director is more interested in your honest connection to the character than in whether you flub a line or miss a comma. "In real life, people talk about what they know. Not what someone wrote for them." – Stella Adler. Tip: note the page number so you can guesstimate where the scene falls within the arc of the story (teaser, beginning, middle, end.)

3. If it's available, read the script. If not, Plan B is to download the other character sides from the project or episode and read theirs in addition to yours. Sometimes this will reveal new information about the story or your character that isn't in your pages. Also read any parts of the pages that have been marked through by casting with a black marker. Every once in a while there is a clue buried in there as well.

4. If you can't pronounce it, ask. If you don't understand it, look it up. Two excellent sites for looking up pronunciation are howjsay.com and forvo.com.

5. Do not neglect the stage directions! Actors eager to get off-book make the mistake of focusing on just the dialogue. Most of the circumstances (who, what, where, when) and clues to the character are contained in the

stage directions themselves, shaping the depth, tone, pace, and tension of the scene. The writer has given you a gift. Use it.

6. Know your form, know your audience. Accept the form, accept the audience. Watch episodes or previous films by the writer/director in order to understand their style, taste, and genre. Some television is simply meant to be fun and distracting, and it's written that way, so don't force your "method" on the form. Common sense tells you that if you dive head first in to shallow waters, you're likely to break your neck.

7. Walk in with confidence, grace, and purpose. A professional who's ready to work has a pleasant and businesslike demeanor. Acknowledge the auditors, but don't shake their hands. Hit your standing mark or go to the chair. They'll ask if you're ready, you'll nod, take your "moment before," and then begin.

8. Slating your name is usually done only for commercials, not for TV/Film. There are exceptions to this, however. More on this below.

9. Read facing forward and toward the camera as much as possible. Because "the eyes are the windows of the soul," you want your face to be seen as much as possible. If the previous actor chose to stand and simply moved the chair away, it may not have been reset for the next actor. If the chair has been awkwardly or unfavorably placed away from the camera, ask to change it. On the rare occasion that the reader is unfavorably placed a few feet away from the lens, find an imaginary spot closer to the lens, and continue to interact with the reader as if they were there. Remember that if you can't see the lens, it can't see you.

10. You can assume that a taped audition will be shot in either a medium close or tighter close-up. If you want to make sure, ask about the framing.

11. Seated or standing? Seated is preferable because many auditions are now put "to tape," and this keeps you grounded and in frame, minimizing large, physical gestures and nervous tics not appropriate for the scene. But sometimes the audition is standing, and you won't know that until you enter. At home, rehearse it both ways in case a chair is not available. You want to feel comfortable and self-disciplined in both situations. If the scene needs physicality, find an easy freedom of movement by rotating on your axis, and use that instead of lateral moves forward and sideways that throw you out of frame.

12. Sit upright in the middle of the chair, toward the edge. It keeps your posture and energy up and gives you more flexibility and freedom if you physicalize your characterization. When you sit back fully, the spine collapses a bit, trapping or sapping your energy and spontaneity. Do not lean forward, resting on your knees, because you'll look like a no-neck hunchback on camera. If this is a physical character choice, fine, but the dramatic effect is useful for only a few seconds, and then you'll need to adjust your position so that you're more favorably seen and heard.

13. Float your pages in front of you, chest high and a little flat. Do not cover your face. Do not put pages in your lap. Do not hold them to your side. This frontal placement of the pages will minimize "the nodding dog" and "the bobblehead doll." You want your pages where you can naturally avert only your eyes or use slight tilts of the head when picking up a line you need. They want to see your eyes and face as much as possible. Pages should be held with a light, easy command, without stiffness or tension.

14. Hold your pages, even if you are off-book. Sure, a professional is a quick study and gives a fully prepared audition, freely interacting at performance level. But every working professional knows to keep their pages in their hands. Why? On the off chance you go up on

your lines, you won't be naked and stumbling. The pages will be there to troubleshoot the moment. Holding your pages also indicates that you are not locked into or "married" to a performance, which tells the director that there is still room to influence your choices.

15. If this is a cold reading, work off the page and act "off" the page. This is still an acting audition, so don't become completely absorbed in the script by literally reading it. Bring the words up and out.

16. Take your "moment before" to transition from yourself into the character and dynamics of the scene, then make eye contact with the reader. This takes only a few seconds, and is most important and should not be skipped. Amateurs make the mistake of going straight to the words without this transition, and it often weakens their performance. Taking the moment before establishes chemistry with the reader (as the character), and grounds you in the conflict of the scene. Do this before you say a single word. Draw that person into the scene with you. You can maintain chemistry in their dialogue by continuing eye contact, actively listening, and visually responding to what they're saying. Relax – let their words be new; you're still in character even when you don't have dialogue. The auditors will want to see your understanding of the character, the scene, and truthful exchange – *not* memorized words and planned reactions. Don't just "show" that you're listening, but really listen.

ACTING TIP: Every once in a while, the transition for the moment before can be best served with a small, physical gesture - one that is in keeping with the character and will throw you in to the emotional seat of the scene. This is especially helpful when the top of the scene is obviously in the middle of an argument or a bombshell of some kind has landed before the first line. But don't let the gesture disconnect the chemistry with your reader and be played as two separate beats – both must be seamlessly layered as one moment.

17. For strong, emotional scenes on camera, work deeper and not bigger. The deeper and more connected you are, the less likely you are to engage in over-the-top physicality or tension-based tics (panting, swaying, jiggling feet) that have nothing to do with the character. Actually, the deeper you work, the larger your "inner size" becomes, which naturally radiates the power of your heart and soul outward. You won't need the big displays of "schmacting" and planning your beats – that's for amateurs. Love your work, love your character, focus on that, and you'll forget how nervous you are. Tension is the actor's greatest enemy.

18. Acting "off the page" refers to the technique of handling your pages when you're not completely off-book. Remember, these reading tips are for the short-notice audition. If you're not completely off-book, the first thing to do is to stop worrying. Instead, use your pages and act "off the page." This means you stay in character as you are reading, pick up your next line(s) from the page, and bring your face up toward the camera as often as you can while speaking. Continue your connection to the scene without interrupting the flow and pace of the writing.

19. In readings with long speeches, some actors (including me) use a technique of "bookending." The actor knows the first line of a speech, and the last line, and is able to give both of those off-book, fully to the reader and camera without looking at the script. Bookending this way keeps the speech visually strong for the camera when there's little time to prepare, and you can still act off the page for the body of the speech. This is a skill you can attain with practice.

20. Do not look into the camera lens during your scene, ever, unless specifically requested to by the director, or if the script is purposely written to break the fourth

wall, like *Ferris Bueller's Day Off*. On occasion, if there is more than one character you must play to in the scene, you may choose to look directly to the left/right of the camera instead of directly at your reader. Practice at home beforehand to plan your eye lines.

21. You can look directly at the reader as the other character, but not at any other casting person or production team member. Production creatives need to maintain a neutral eye and will not be able to if you break the fourth wall by using them in your scene. It makes them self-conscious. On the rare occasion they happen to be sitting where you'd planned to use an eyeline, simply choose another spot over their shoulder, or look at the wall space directly above their heads.

22. Casting directors write notes during readings. It's not personal. It's their job. Let them do their job. They could be writing something fabulous.

23. If your character is part of the love interest, look for moments of spontaneity and electricity. Beyond just passion, a lover is often grateful, appreciative, and committed. What if there is a kiss? Often in films, the most exciting part of the kiss is the hesitation and moment before contact, and the releasing effect of it afterwards. For the audition, make the kiss itself brief and close-mouthed, then play the effects of the kiss afterward for the real moment of your scene. Did it make you blush? Surprised? Confused? Outraged? Or did you melt? The icky audition kiss occurs when the actor makes the moment *about the kiss itself*, open-mouthed and twirling the tongue to empty air. This looks raunchy and ridiculous – a huge turn-off. The auditor will be stuck on that instead of staying involved with the remainder of the scene.

24. Do not worry about a muffed line. Stay in character and refuse to let that worry or distract you. In some cases, it can even be viewed as a "happy accident," a

character choice. On the rare occasion when you know you're unfocused or have started badly, stop immediately. Politely and without apology, ask to start again. They probably won't let you start the audition over if you finish the whole scene (badly) before asking for another try. Even if they do, the first impression is already tarnished. When starting again, take a brief beat to center yourself, take your acting "moment before," and deliver with concentration and focus. Pick your battles and shrink things to the right size – not every flub is a disastrous mistake. A lot of film pros trip up on lines, blithely take a beat, and start again without cutting and resetting the take because it saves time and energy on the set.

25. When finished, you can ask if there are any adjustments. If so, take the note and change your performance – even if you disagree. Sometimes, it's just a test to see if you are flexible and can take direction. If there are none, thank them and leave with the same confidence, grace, and good spirit you came in with. On your exit, do not apologize or negatively comment on your own performance in any way – save your insecurity for the drive home.

THE CALLBACK – *"If it ain't broke, don't fix it."*

A callback is when an actor is asked to return to read for the same role after production has narrowed their choices. It is also known as a "Producer Session." Unless you're told otherwise, do what you did in the first interview. Do not remodel your character or dismantle your original ideas. Hone and develop it, yes, but don't abandon it (including your wardrobe.) They called you back because they liked something you brought to the role. If you radically change your approach, you might lose the one thing that won you the callback.

FOR THE CO-STAR AND 5-and-UNDERS
"Work clean."

These are sometimes the hardest roles to play because they have the fewest lines and information. The tendency for the amateur player is to "milk them," overanalyze, or impose phony plots not intended by the writer – three lines turn into three acts.

Know that sometimes the only function of this character is to move the plot forward, or set the pace and timing for the next scene – and you need to accept that responsibility. You can still be authentic, imaginative, funny, and spontaneous, but you must simplify your timing by using highly specific visualization that will provoke quick, emotional responses ("work clean".)

The only time you might work any differently on a role of this size is in the rare circumstance that the breakdown states it is a "POSSIBLE RECURRING." In this instance, you are not imposing a phony plot or non-existent relationships. For these occasions, absolutely do your homework to fill yourself and those moments with a richer past and higher stakes.

Take heart, my co-stars. Everyone starts here. I did. A job well done by a newcomer they took a chance on will lead to more appointments and bigger roles. Casting directors often work several shows at a time, and a good first impression is a great way to get on their radar.

THE EXTERNALS
Wardrobe: Dress appropriately "toward" the role, as a suggestion – not full costume. Ladies, beware of short skirts. They ride up even more when seated, making it hard for the auditors to focus on your face and talent.

Makeup: Ladies, wear just enough to polish and enhance your looks; use heavier makeup only if appropriate to the character. For men, none at all. Do wash your face or blot with tissue to reduce shine on camera. For both genders, avoid perfume and cologne altogether.

Accents: Do not use an accent unless you can do it excellently – develop understanding of the scene and character first, accent last.

Props: Woe to the actor with a bag of tricks. It's best if you can do the reading entirely without props. If you believe you must, then choose simple items (such as a pen or glasses), and use them sparingly. Your scene should never depend on a desired effect that only a prop can give. They should be used only to enhance a moment, not take over the scene.

ON SLATING YOUR NAME

Slating is generally used only for commercial auditions, not for television or film. If you were to automatically give a commercial slate in a TV/Film audition, you'd be committing a faux pas; it's an indication that you're green. However, there *are* some exceptions:

1. Filming a TV or film audition scene with the intention of sending that link by email (Eco-Casts, Pre-Reads and out-of-state productions)

2. If you are unrepresented talent, and an agent or manager has not arranged the appointment

3. If you are a youth or teen new to the market and just starting your career

Typically in these instances, TV/Film casting posts very specific instructions regarding slates for the actor beforehand, so look for them in the breakdown or the appointment notice. For the slate: at the top, you'll state your name and the role you're reading for, then give yourself a couple of seconds to transition into your character and begin the scene. Sometimes they will instruct you to give your agency name, or hold a sheet of paper with your name legibly written plus a contact number. Some will ask the actor to add a "tail slate" at the end as well. For the tail slate, the actor stands after the scene is over and repeats the "slate" from the opening. The camera zooms out to full frame, then pans down and back up for the body shot. The audition itself is normally shot in a "loose medium" frame (mid-chest to above the hairline), and seated. However, independent electronic auditions are not the norm. Most of the time, the actor will audition in person for casting and production, and for these, you do not slate.

OTHER TIPS

• Be on time – in fact, be early. You never know when you'll be greeted by a new set of sides or copy. Anticipate your time: traffic, weather, and parking (with plenty of quarters in your car for meters.)

• Stay attentive and quiet in the waiting room. If an actor wants to distract you with a conversation, ask if they'll be around afterward so you can talk to them later.

• Be polite to the casting assistants. Today's assistant is tomorrow's casting director.

• Know who's in the room and the number of people you'll be reading for. You can ask the casting assistant when you arrive, or ask other actors as they exit. Sometimes producers and directors are busy shooting, and they cast off the callback tape, so don't pout if there's only a couple of folks and a camera. If there are several (as for network tests and producer sessions), don't allow the number of people in the room to surprise you.

• Once in the room, don't waste anyone's time with your lengthy actor warm-up or breathing exercises.

• Stay focused on the scene and allow nothing in the room to distract you – not eating, phone calls, conversation, inattentiveness, or rudeness – not even a lousy reading partner. Use your talent and imagination and act as if they are giving you exactly what you need. Play the life and the reality of the scene, not the life and reality of the room.

• I prefer to make strong choices in circumstance and emotion beforehand, and go for it in the audition. Feel free to ask brief questions about the story and character, but avoid discussing the character at length. It's still about acting, not chatting them up. If you are confused, ask simple questions, find out what they want, then go for it to the best of your ability.

THE RIDE, NOT THE ROTE

BREAKING DOWN THE SCRIPT AND CHARACTER DEVELOPMENT FOR TV/FILM AUDITIONS

In the previous section, the audition technique was about the business and technical side of the audition room itself. Next, we apply your craft and artistry to the needs of your material, which gets tricky when you're given short notice and you're tempted to rote memorize instead of apply it. You still need the wisdom and sensitivity of your acting training for the performance – you just prioritize your choices when there's little time to prepare. Don't get impatient and cheat the process - there are no shortcuts. There may not be shortcuts, but there are breakthroughs, and the actor picks up speed and acuity. This only comes with time and patience.

OVERALL APPROACH

1. BE PRECISE IN THE TOTAL PHYSICAL LIFE OF THE SCENE, and make strong choices on the psychological and emotional aspects of your character and their relationships therein. Some actors choose "safe" because they are either mediocre, uninformed, or afraid of risk. Stay honest, personal, and logical to the scene, and don't forget to find the moments of charm and humor, even in drama. "In your choices lies your talent," said Stella Adler. "If your choices reside in the middle, so does your talent."

2. BE SPECIFIC AND HIGHLY visual through your creative imagination with the facts of the script.

Visualization is the key – see it, see everything. If you can see it, we can see it.

3. FOR COMEDY, DO NOT CHANGE ONE WORD! An extra syllable or word change, even an "um" could kill a joke. Jokes are built on rhythm and pace and the writer has been deliberate in these choices. Hell hath no fury like a comedy writer misquoted.

4. FOR ALL COMEDY, "WORK CLEAN." Let your timing and bits have precision.

5. NO "SCHMACTING." NO PLANNING YOUR MOMENTS. Let it unfold, without effort, as if it's all for the first time. The actor always knows more than the characters themselves, but the character doesn't know what's coming next.

6. ON CAMERA, "LESS IS MORE." You don't need to "show us," or push your instrument if the thought and emotion are strong and genuinely present. The camera sees everything, and every movement is magnified. Theatre is a physical medium, but the camera is a visual one.

UNDERSTANDING versus ROTE MEMORIZATION

Start now to develop good habits or replace the superficial ones. Production creatives are looking for the human connection to the scene, not your ability to spout a perfect word count. I've been doing this approach for so long now that I now work automatically with good habits – hard, fast, and deep – resulting in rather consistent success. Very little time is given to us to learn material for auditions. Over time, you too will develop taste in prioritizing which choices demand your full attention first, but all circumstances of the script and character should be thoughtfully considered. The more you practice these methods and suggestions, the easier it gets, and without much memorization. Here's a thought: two hundred other actors are going to be rote memorizing their lines. You can easily turn into just another guy in jeans and a V-neck, or just another girl with a hairdo and heels. The best plan for any professional is to *dig out the script first and learn the lines last,* not the other way around (as in rote memorization first, then imposing a meaning later.)

My road experience has consistently supported the lesson that when I deepened my understanding first, it automatically helped me learn my lines, faster and more efficiently, while enriching both my inner life and my inner size. So, repeat after me: understanding first, memorizing last. I apply this approach to all of my projects and auditions, within all limitations of time for prep, be it a month, a week, or a day, including my auditions for TV and film.

Are there exceptions to this? Yes, there can be. There are some situations with a lot of text and a next-to-nothing time for rehearsal. These are outside the norm and may surprise or alarm an actor, increasing their temptation to reverse the process and memorize first. Here are a few such situations that I've worked in that presented this dilemma: soap operas; summer stock; classics in verse; procedural roles that have complicated scientific or medical terminology (common in one-hour dramas for television); commercial copy, infomercial and industrial auditions; emergency replacement of an actor; foreign or regional slang that is unfamiliar but packed with specific meaning or humor in translation; and overnight bookings and shoots.

The common denominators here are large volumes of text, no rehearsal time, and writing with a complicated or unconventional vocabulary. *I consider "large" a full script, not a four-page audition scene.* Even with 11 to 15 pages to prepare for an audition, I still break down and dig out the script first as much as I can. I know this is my key to finding a character worth looking at while using the technique of working "off the page."

Even under these circumstances, we must coordinate the learning with making ourselves and circumstances real, giving the acting substance. If you go straight to the words, the danger is that you will kill inspiration, fall into the bad habit of line readings, and fail to truly listen and respond. The end result looks phony and planned. The biggest trap of rote memorization is that you'll be "locked." You won't be able to let go of your choices, which is often the reason you'll freeze and "go up" on your lines when you try something fresh. It is also the reason an actor is unable to change direction if given an adjustment in the audition.

I go to the words to inspire my mind, which triggers the gut (instinct), which provokes a need to speak, and the words come out. And that's the proper relationship of the actor to the word: words > thought > experience > need > back to the word. No one can tell you when a thought ends and the word begins, because it happens in a flash. Script breakdown isn't a cold, intellectual exercise, like a book report, where actors are in danger of being trapped in their heads. Understanding is a function of the heart, not the mind. Think of it this way: when you dig out a garden, you get your hands dirty. When you dig out a script, you get your heart dirty. You create a little chaos inside yourself. It can feel very uncomfortable, even painful, during the process. But not all chaos is bad, and chaos is always temporary. Summon your curiosity and give yourself permission to live in the mystery of the unanswered question.

I often go to a Zen saying I love that captures script breakdown more simply: "I hear and I forget. I see and I remember. I do and I understand." To act is "to do." It is my first duty as an actor to understand, and allow myself to be moved by that understanding. Throw your heart and the body will follow.

So let us begin with techniques to replace rote memorization. The following script breakdown is in line with that of the full script breakdown process, but has been condensed for television and film auditions. It is also quite useful for scene study classes. A full and complete script breakdown can take anywhere from 2 to 6 weeks to complete. It is most necessary for leading roles in big plays and screenplays, but impractical and overwhelming for the short-form audition. I learned these career-changing techniques directly from the late, great Stella Adler, and I consider them my greatest survival tools.

SCRIPT AND CHARACTER BREAKDOWN FOR TV/FILM

"The difficult becomes habit. The habit becomes easy. The easy, beautiful." - Sergei Volkonsky

Use the following outline and you will begin to experience the extraordinary reversal of the play working you, not you working the play. Answer and develop what you can, with the time and information you're given. Fulsome research needs time management, so if the audition scene relies on it, needs it, then do it. But, if it's just a side issue, prioritize your focus and energy on the primary elements that drive the scene and character for the audition.

Also, in the beginning, do not focus only on the emotional life of the scene, there is much more to the human experience than easy anger or tears. We should never pressure ourselves to cry on cue – the more you chase an emotion, the less likely you are to have it. Instead, find and develop as much of the physical life, the total life of the scene as you can, because this may actually provide natural triggers. Baiting your emotions through circumstances such where you are, or the character's past, may very well be the key to the effortless expression of an emotional life.

Before you begin, remember to read the script, or as many other character sides posted for casting, as possible. Also remember to search the stage directions for the clues and answers to the questions below.

1) NAME THE SCENE. For example: the marriage proposal, the interrogation, the seduction, the fight, the practical joke.

2) THE PAST. Look for everything in the text, including the stage directions, that mentions the past, and creatively build on it. "Was, were, -ed" statements.

   a) The past can be the moment before, an immediate/recent past, or a more distant biographical past. We must see a person in *continuation* of their life.

   b) In order to start the scene with a strong "moment before," you'll need to know the immediate past and what just happened. You will fail if you go straight to the words without the grounding moment before.

3) PLOTLINE – list only the major events of the scene.

4) IDENTIFY THE CIRCUMSTANCES, i.e. THE FACTS. These are the Who, What, Where, When, How, Why of the script, basic Stanislavsky. Find them in the script, and then enlarge them through research and creative imagination. Ask yourself the following:

   a) WHO am I? Begin now to speak in first person about yourself as the character.

    i) You can find these in the "I," "me," "mine" statements of your dialogue in the script.

    ii) How are you described in the breakdown, stage directions, or statements by other characters? For instance, being called lazy, a bitch, or suspicious may or may not be true, but will definitely inform and shape your choices in delivery. Look for "you," "yours," "he," "she" types of statements in others' dialogue.

    iii) Does your name mean anything? (Sometimes it's deliberate and a clue.)

    iv) Who are you talking to? What are they to you – friend or foe?

    v) Animals – if your character has been described as one, study its mannerisms and, if there's time, subtly blend them into your physical presence or tone.

b) WHERE am I? Every place has mood, tension, and a physical life. See it in detail, with great specificity, and be able to move within it imaginatively and respond to the place.

c) WHAT am I? Important when it drives the scene or is central to the character. Prioritize and use as needed.

    i) Profession

    ii) Class distinction: upper/middle/blue collar etc.

    iii) Gender and family: mother, father, daughter, son, etc. and stage of life/age

    iv) Religious, political, or belief system

d) WHEN? (time of day, time in history, seasons)

e) WHY? Establishes need. Why are you saying this? Why are you doing this? Be patient, as subtext and need are revealed in time. Just continue to ask why until you get down the essential idea, the one you cannot do without in order to justify your actions and speech.

5) FIND THE CONFLICT: Keep it short and simple when considering the objectives, obstacles, and what's at stake. What do I want? What do they want from me? What's in my way? What will happen if I don't get it?

6) CHARACTER ARC: Subtly or significantly, your character always begins in one state of mind or being, changes during the events of the scene, and ends in a different state of mind or being.

7) Find THE EMOTIONAL LIFE OF THE SCENE, then find THE EMOTIONAL TRUTH OF YOUR CHARACTER.

a) For instance, you might name the scene "A Wake" and the emotional life of the whole scene could be one of grief. But the emotional truth of your character is singular – not everyone grieves the same way. Your character is an individual. Caution: Do not confuse this with your personal truth. There is you, and then there is the play. If your method involves substitutions, use them to trigger and initiate, but enlarge on them imaginatively to justify the character as written. Serve the character, serve the play.

8) REFINE EACH BEAT found with the large events of the plotline. These can happen very quickly in TV/Film, and are only meant to give the scene shape and structure.

a) Beats can be found by looking for: the introduction of a brand new idea or discovery stated for the first time, the "game changer"; the interruption of the scene as with an entrance/exit of a character, a bomb blast or a telephone ring that suddenly breaks the dialogue; and/or, sustained actions/ "doings", (the beginning and completion of an activity during a particular run of dialogue), that often bookend a beat.

❖ KNOWING THE PLOTLINE, BEATS, AND CHARACTER ARC IS VERY IMPORTANT, ESPECIALLY WHEN YOU BOOK. Why? Because they shoot out of sequence. If you are clear within yourself about these elements, it will be easier to pick up the thread of the story and continue the heat of the moment that leads into the new "set-up" of the camera.

9) FIND THE ACTION(S): This is the HOW of circumstances. Be on the hunt for actions, not just emotions. An actor can get either bogged down or over animated, so be careful with this part. You do not have to know your action first before you rehearse the scene. It's likely that you'll discover the action as you work.

a) In a nutshell: an action is "to do" something, as in to protect, to destroy, to escape.

b) Actions can be physical, psychological, verbal, or emotional – by themselves or in combination.

c) In the world of full script breakdown, overall actions pertain to the play, main actions pertain to the scene, and immediate actions pertain to the moment-by-moment activities and beats within the scene. For the purpose of auditions, focus on just the main action of your scene, then the major beats that shift the story into a beginning, middle, and end.

d) "Activities" are small physical actions, often using props, that can interfere and get in the way of an audition scenario – and I normally save those for the shoot. If you feel compelled to do otherwise, then be very specific, very natural, and very brief. If you can't do it well, don't do it at all for an audition.

10) FIND THE TARGET OF YOUR EYELINE: Visualize and place each person or object you're speaking to or about in the script. This will automatically radiate and realistically shift both the distance perspective of your

eyeline, and your energy outward to the right point during your dialogue. Are you speaking to yourself? The other character? The audience or landscape? The universe? Notice that the natural energy of the first placement to yourself is intimate, self-contained, sometimes played as a "throwaway" and then the energy grows outward in size accordingly, filling the space between you and each successive point. This is very important when establishing eyelines for camera, and maintaining the logic of your exchanges with other characters. This kind of conscious attention in the beginning will subtly shift your emotional and mental actions – more fun to play, more fun to watch.

11) CHOOSE SIMPLE AND SPECIFIC BODY LANGUAGE. After considering the who, where, what of your character, play with how any one of those elements might affect your walk, posture, or attack of speech – if at all. Sometimes exploring an animal's gait and mannerism is needed. But remember that "less is more" in TV and film and it's not needed for every role.

12) REFINE YOUR DELIVERY: Look for any words or ideas that do not reside "in the middle," but are in a heightened state of being. For example:

a) Large Words = now, never, forever, always, nothing, vast, desolate, inconsolable, hostile, terrified, riveting, bombastic, effervescent, torrid, howling, garish, sacred.

b) Large Ideas = peace, war, death, children, hope, love, struggle, freedom, humanity, truth, greed, immortality, redemption.

c) Large Subtext = metaphor, satire, double meanings, sexual innuendo, irony, sarcasm.

13) DEVELOP THE SURPRISES: Some surprises and reversals are big and demand that you play the moment; others demand subtlety and are more powerful when thrown away or covered up.

14) PUT THE SCRIPT DOWN AND PLAY THE SCENE as well as you can remember. Paraphrasing during this final part of the process is natural, but you should be able to play the entire scene as written with most of the ideas and actions in place. Go back and work on the places in the script where you dropped a line – it means you dropped your understanding. Revisit that moment, explore it more, and begin to work more precisely with the text as written.

15) THROW YOUR WORK AWAY. In the end, after you've done the work and learned the dialogue, then trust that it's in you. You put it there, after all, and it can now work as muscle memory – actor muscle. Just stay loose and flexible. Remember, the actor knows what's next, but the character doesn't. Say everything, think everything, see everything, and hear everything as if for the first time. It's called "being in the moment."

If you can't find the answer to every single question right away, don't worry, not everything is possible to know in a few pages and a few hours. Simply move on to the next indicated thing. Keep working with the time and the tools you are given. As you continue to deepen your understanding of and familiarity with the humanity of the scene, more will be revealed – the answers will come, and so will the words.

A WORD ABOUT BEATS

If you have not had a lot of technique or training, "beats" may confuse and sidetrack you, so you may want to skip this until you've had more time with your coach. If you have had technique and training, this next section may clarify some things.

Beats have often been described as "thoughts" – well, yes and no. Eventually, yes. But if you approach the script in the very beginning with this in mind, each individual thought and moment will overwhelm you, because you don't understand the larger scene first. So, keep this part *very simple* for the audition scene and break it down first into large beats, then smaller and smaller beats until it finally becomes the stream of consciousness (thoughts) that allows you to play the scene "in the moment." For instance, in playing each consecutive moment (thought), I might very well pull on my pants, button my shirt, and tie my shoes, but they all fall within the logic of one large beat: to get dressed.

Beats can also confuse and trap an actor into thinking too much, so it's important that you *"Wear it like a loose coat,"* as my coach use to say, because the beats are temporary and meant to be used only in the early stages of rehearsals. Once you are in performance mode, they must merge and become seamless – we are not supposed to see your work. Their purpose is to give the text simple structure and give the actor manageable bites of the script to chew. Stanislavski's wisdom: "The larger and fewer the divisions, the easier for you to handle the whole scene." He likened the script to a turkey – you'd choke if you swallowed it whole. And, you don't plop the whole turkey on your plate (the play, the scene) and then dig it out a forkful at a time (thoughts.) You must first cut the turkey into sections, then into smaller portions, and then cut those into bite-sized morsels.

Large beats are units, chunks, a collective group of the same thoughts/actions/events. Giving each one a name can also be helpful in keeping these separate and simple. There are always clues in the script that indicate a beat change. So, again, be on the lookout for:

1. the introduction of a brand new idea or discovery stated for the first time: the "game changer"

2. the sudden interruption of the scene with an entrance/exit of a character, a bomb blast, or a

telephone ring that suddenly breaks the dialogue

3. sustained actions or "doings" (the beginning and completion of an activity during a particular run of dialogue) that often bookend a beat.

REHEARSAL TECHNIQUES

THE ART OF PARAPHRASING

Paraphrasing is often used in early stages of preparation for the role and is really excellent for monologues. It requires that you put the big themes and ideas of the writer, and the character's dialogue, into your own words, and then be able to clearly communicate that to someone else. This allows you as an actor to get closer to the role, physically, emotionally, and psychologically, without the hiccup on every word you "drop."

Read the full scene aloud, both parts, including stage directions, several times. Then read just your part aloud, silently reading the other characters. Read all of it lightly and easily, just let the words roll out so you can hear the pace and rhythm of the scene. *Do not interpret yet*, because you are still working "cold." Interpretation comes later while you're breaking down the script.

Next, begin breaking down the script by gathering and exploring the facts of the scene. Once you feel your understanding deepen, put the dialogue in your own words, paragraph by paragraph, or line by line.

Return to the original text, including the stage directions, and visualize everything – go through the sentences as sequences of thoughts and imagery. Repeat this until the visual sequences and beats flow with smoothness. Do not memorize the words, but feel free to begin to incorporate them, paraphrasing easily in and around the actual text.

Dig out the beats, the defining moments, reveals, and action where the scene turns in a big, new direction. Move through the build and overall growth, deepening your paraphrase to use as subtext. Note the breaks in the tension. Repeat this until it feels natural.

Using your own words in full paraphrase, tell it to someone else and see whether you're able to fully communicate the ideas and sequences of thought of the text. Do this in rehearsals on your own time, not in the waiting room.

Now you can begin the down-and-dirty duty of memorizing/learning your lines. Return to the text as written and fill the words with your understanding. Do this until it feels natural and you *know* the text. At this point, the combined work of paraphrasing with script breakdown should yield surprisingly good – and effortless – first runs of the actual text. It might be a little rough around the edges, you might not be entirely "off book," but about 90 percent of it will be there. Anything you don't know will still flow when working "off the page" in the audition.

In all ways, we must serve the writer, serve the playwright. Do not fall in love with your paraphrase and rewrite the scene during the audition – the writer and director want to hear the text as written. A wise mentor of mine warned, *"The flower of improvisation blooms only once."* Paraphrasing is an exercise, a kind of improv, and is there to enlarge our experience of the script, not to replace it. This early work begins slowly, so be patient; you will eventually increase your tempo to meet the demands of pace and rhythm which are always present in television and film script.

ACTIVATING THE PAST

Go back through the script and find the clues to the past. There are influential events and character elements that are mentioned, but not necessarily enacted, within the scene, and you can find these by looking for "was," "were," and "-ed" at the end of words. Since there is a lack of time for auditions, be practical and thoughtful and choose only vital elements. By fully engaging and exploring the past, you will actually create experiences for the character's "sense memory," instead of relying solely on your personal past. Substitutions are fine as a starting place, but can and should be imaginatively enlarged to justify the character as an individual.

The upcoming exercises are particularly helpful for leads, supporting leads, guest stars, and recurring contracts. Not all roles have the size to warrant an in-depth activation for an audition situation, and not all of the exercises below have to be done. Develop the taste and instinct to choose the defining moments of your character – moments that drive the scene – and then choose the exercises below that make the most sense. Spend the time to give it life and color.

WORK ON A CHARACTER BIOGRAPHY: Do not arbitrarily make one up. Use the facts and clues given in the script. Many insights can be had, for instance, by fully considering the milestones in the life of that character: a mother and child; the poverty of the Great Depression; how your outlook was shaped by living in the Deep South; or the vivid detail of the day your father disappeared.

For stories regarding loss through death or divorce, the actor trap is to go for the loss and squeeze the instrument for tears. The secret to grief and loss is this:

build a life worth losing. Before you focus on the loss, experience the really great things from that relationship. For instance, the loss of a husband: the moment you fell in love, the first kiss, laughing over a practical joke, your first stupid argument, the smell of his clothes in the closet, and the curve of his neck. If you can find the joy and magic, the adventure or simple contentment of love, then the torment of parting takes cares of itself. It takes no effort at all for tears to rise to the occasion. And you do this by imaginatively building a past.

CHASE THE IMAGE: If you have a fluid imagination, this is a beautiful exercise. Simply start with the facts, let an image in full color and place emerge, and allow the story to unfold. If another character enters, follow them through the room and see where they take you.

For instance, I once played a role as a mother who'd lost her 22-year-old daughter in a terrible accident. Facts of the Script: Mother. Daughter. Death. Love. Actor's Challenge? Build a life worth losing. All Mothers remember the milestones in the life of their child: the first step, their first words, years and seasons of "firsts." I placed myself in a quiet, secluded room. The image came that I was in a bedroom I'd never seen before, folding clothes on a bed I'd never owned. There was soft morning light swimming past sheer curtains hung on the window. From a dark hallway, bare feet slapped against the wood, and a little freckle-faced brunette in a pink nightgown played peek-a-boo with me from the corner. She was giddy and tangled, and pointed to her smile, sticking her tongue through the gap – she had just lost her first tooth. I had created a sweet and indelible memory in a mother's life – all fresh, all new, to justify the character's 'sense memory,' not relying upon my own experience as a mother with a daughter.

RE-ENACTMENT: Place yourself at the events mentioned but not shown in the script. Play them out with your imagination, write them out, even put them on their feet if it's legal and you're able.

PERSONAL MOMENT: This is an intimate activity, and singular to your character. Fully and physically explore an activity that your character would do when alone. For example, Laura from *The Glass Menagerie* polished her little glass animals. They all had names, personalities, and history. The act itself allowed Laura to leave this world and enter into a kind of magic bubble, a world of her making, a world that was safe.

PRIVATE MOMENT: A private moment is similar to a personal moment, except the character would stop immediately if someone entered the room. Our private face is different from our public face. For instance, Laura probably wouldn't stop polishing the animals for Tom or Amanda. It was personal, but not private. They'd seen her do it many times and allowed her the comfort of doing so. A private moment must be so deeply private, like a secret, that we'd be mortified if it were witnessed.

MOMENT BEFORE: This is useful for all actors, regardless of the size of the part. The moment before is about the immediate past and events that happened *before the top of the scene*. It affects all entrances and the first line of dialogue. When done well, the audience sees a person in continuation of their life in real time. When done badly, we see an actor waiting for a cue.

At best what we see during a scene is only a fraction of the total truth of the character – the total truth remains in you. It is the same in life. We are ourselves with our own individual pasts, but we display only a fraction of the total truth to the world at any given time. The actor can reveal only a small part of the character's past, created according to the demands of the scene, but the actor owns and carries that entire past of the character. It is still in you, still colors the entire performance, but it won't be in you unless you put it there first. Ownership of the work comes with responsibilities, and you have to work for it.

COMMERCIAL CASTING CALLS

Show up early to learn copy. Sometimes copy is posted electronically through your audition notice. After arrival and parking, find the designated studio inside the casting house that will host the product for your audition. Most houses are casting more than one ad. From there, you will sign-in: first, by writing it on the sheet in the waiting room, and then again electronically in the audition room by the session runner.

ELECTRONIC SIGN-IN

Currently, most commercial auditions utilize an electronic sign-in for actors. It begins when you confirm your audition online at home through the audition notice in your email. Once confirmed, your information is held, and double confirmed by the session runner before you slate inside the audition room itself. Confirming online with the casting service is not enough – you must also confirm separately with your agent or manager by email.

With casting houses working through Casting Frontier, a bar code is the alternative electronic sign-in procedure. A computer is often available in the casting waiting room for you to access your bar code, but I find it easier to print it at home beforehand. Your bar code will then be scanned moments before the session starts.

THE SIGN-IN SHEET

Sign in with your name, your Union ID number (not your social security number), agency initials, time of arrival, time of audition, and whatever else the form asks of you: 1st/2nd call, gender M/F, age -40/+40, etc. There is a box you initial *after* your audition is over, verifying the time in and time out. This enables you to get paid if your audition holds you for an unreasonable length of time, or goes to numerous callbacks. This is a Union provision designed to protect you from being held hostage by the session. This is a highly unusual occurrence, but it does happen.

Pick up a copy of the copy (script), and read the board above the sign-in table. It will give you additional information on the callback and shooting dates. Then read the storyboard, if available, to see how the agency has visually blocked this commercial for the shoot. It may give you a better idea of the style and humor of the campaign.

Most calls will take an electronic "snapshot" of you inside the room during your slate, and your regular profile has already been sent through Casting Networks or Casting Frontier. Your "size sheets" are also part of your online site pages, and not usually filled out anymore. Because of this, many casting rooms no longer ask for headshots, resumes, and size sheets, but do bring an extra headshot and resume to callbacks. Ad agencies and clients (the product) sometimes like to have them in their hands, so bring one or two headshots to callbacks, just in case.

THE COPY

ACTING TIP: USE THE CORK. Crisp speech in commercial copy and voice-over work is important, so warm up at home or in the car with a cork to help with muddy speech on morning calls, or with copy that's particularly heavy in technical language and tongue-twisters. Place the tip of the cork between your teeth, and o-ver e-nun-ci-ate ev-er-y syl-la-ble. It makes your mouth tired, but every p, t, d, k sound will be easily said and heard. Do this privately. The waiting room is not the place.

Study the copy, and learn or memorize as much as you can. Yes, with commercials, you probably need to memorize. However, I still look for the growth in the storyline with a beginning-middle-end. I also consider the audience (demographic) that the product is trying to reach and whether or not my character is a member of that audience. Do I represent (as the character) all women out there just like me? Having wit and good timing is important for many commercial spots, as is natural ease. Lastly, never forget that the client/product IS the story and the most important character in that scene.

The copy will also be inside the session room, on a large board in large print just off-camera for you to reference. It's better to be a quick study, but most session runners are aware of the lack of time for prep, so use the board by "acting off the board" if you need to – and don't break character. "Acting off the board" means you are in character, reading and acting the copy to the board, as if it were to camera, and not floating back and forth from the camera to the words. If you float too much, you weaken the quality of the overall performance and risk looking like a bobblehead. Acting off the board is a very good technique for super cold reads. For the cold-reading nightmare when they ask for copy directly to lens, and you're not at all off-book, use the off-the-board technique but try to "bookend"– at least do the first and last lines directly to the lens to make a strong beginning and ending for camera.

THE AUDITION ROOM

The casting director or session runner will tell you where your mark is for camera, give you brief instructions on the scene, and maybe the characteristics/personality of your role. You should already be making these types of decisions while you're in the waiting room learning lines, but most casting people running the session will fill in the blanks moments before you shoot. Just stay flexible and cooperative, and do the best you can. The great equalizer here is that everybody else up for this spot is also handicapped by the same lack of time and preparation.

HIT YOUR MARK. SLATE YOUR NAME. GIVE PROFILES.

Do these if asked – all with an inner smile to make the outer smile genuine. The "Profiles Please" will, astonishingly, throw most actors for a loop. They suddenly get very self-conscious and feel stiff and clumsy. There are just five basic moves: You start full-face to camera, turn to side profile, turn back to camera as you are turning to the other side profile, then back to camera again. See? Easy. Just make effortless eye contact with the lens each time you move back to camera. Keep this simple, smooth, and free of tension. Anytime you give slates and profiles, look at it as a warm handshake, not a tetanus shot.

THE IMPROMPTU "TELL US SOMETHING"

Every so often, the casting director will surprise the actor with questions, sometimes related to the product. For example, "Can you drive a four-wheel-drive; or stick shift and a clutch?" "Are you allergic to dogs?" "Can you speak French?" (If you can speak French or another language, they'll often ask you to do so immediately, so don't lie.) Or, they'll surprise you with a personal one like "What was your favorite vacation?" or "If you wrote a book, what would the title be?"

Occasionally there is also the ever-dreaded, open-ended, "So, tell us something about yourself." No topic, just anything you happen to want to say about yourself. Or, "Tell us three things about yourself." Plenty of actors have tanked a good room by freezing on this unexpected situation, or they reach for an easy out and report on where they were born. (Yawn.) I advise all my professional clients to always be prepared with the following:

- Be ready with a few anecdotes about yourself that are true and interesting, choose one, and be able to talk about it for about 30 seconds. "My favorite vacation was the summer I saved my brother's life ... I was six years old, he was five ..." and so on. If you have a few ready, you can choose one that might best relate to the circumstances and product – but it is not necessary to have product-related stories, just stories that reveal a bit about you as a person.

- Or, have ready a short list of three things that are true, charming, and interesting. I can say things like: "I flew a plane once, I worked my way through college, and I still like to lie in the grass turning clouds into animal shapes." Short, true, personal

131

experiences that are evocative with imagery and positive, emotional charge.

If you're stumped, look at your "special skills" section on your resume; there are plenty of things for you to reveal. Add a grounded sense of wit and clean humor and you'll be fine. I keep these little life stories in my back pocket, always ready for the unpredictable moment of "So, tell us something about yourself." Just be a good sport, stay flexible, and roll with it. It can be fun, if you let it.

DELIVERY

Do the copy to the best of your ability. Some campaigns just want your natural self, others have a heightened character in mind. Most commercials today, though, don't have the old-school hard sell. They want simple and real. After the first take, you may (or may not) be asked to go again, and the casting director or session runner will offer ideas or make adjustments. Take their note, adjust your performance, and do another take. If you don't agree with the note, *do it their way anyway*. If the copy is worrying you, use the board and act off the board. If you flub, you can ask to begin again, but if you flub repeatedly, they'll lose patience. Take a deep breath, and do it again to the best of your ability, but finish no matter what. And don't beat up on yourself if you're terrible – every good actor has a bad day. Decide to learn from the experience and improve your skillset.

If you're doing fine but you messed up a word here or there, it's not a sin, especially if you stayed in character and most of it had a really good flow. In these cases, don't stop a good run, just move through it, keep up your mojo, and finish. Sometime your "mistakes" are actually "happy accidents" that can make the client fall in love with you.

PUT A "BUTTON" ON IT

The idea behind the "button" is to give the piece an ending, instead of letting it linger unresolved. Many times, when the copy doesn't have a natural exit line or action, I try to button it up with a brief, physical gesture, phrase, or witty remark. It must still be in character, logical to the product, and a natural response. Like real buttons, these are small and simple.

EXIT

Thank them. Leave quickly, leave graciously. Pleasant and efficient = professional. Sign out with your exit time and initials on the sign-in sheet, then leave.

TAPING SELF-SUBMISSIONS

Regional film productions, even local productions, often require actors to self-tape and then electronically submit their auditions. Instead of using an eco-cast service, many actors choose to self-tape at home, so it's extremely important that you follow any self-taping instructions given to you, as requirements may vary by Casting. That being said, here are some general guidelines preferred by many.

1. The setting and background of your audition should be as neutral as possible. Don't distract them from your performance with personal effects, dirty walls, or loud artwork.

2. Sound is important. If your equipment's sound quality is weak, invest in an external microphone. Readers should speak in low, appropriate tones. They are closer to the mic, and therefore louder than the actor. You do not want your Reader to distract and overpower your performance – this is your audition, not theirs.

3. Frame your shot from mid-chest to head.

4. Slate directly to lens. State your full name, name of the role, agency affiliation (or method of contacting you), and your location if do you do not live in the area. If a 'tail slate' is requested, this means you will widen the lens after the performance for a full body shot and repeat the same information you gave in the first slate. All slates are done directly to camera and bookend the beginning and end of the scene.

5. When recording the scene, direct your eye contact to the Reader, NOT the lens. Your Reader should be placed right next to the camera. If there are multiple characters, make sure your eyes move from person to person.

6. Having the sides with you on camera is acceptable, but hold the pages chest high. Lowering your head to read the material in your lap, hides your face and production won't select you if they can't see your talent. It is best to be off-book, if you can.

7. Do not cut tape too soon. Abrupt endings tend to make them think they didn't get the full scene. Land your last line and let it linger a couple of seconds; give it subtext with a thought or reaction (even if the Reader has the last line).

8. Specific wardrobe is not required but consider dressing "toward" the character or body type. Limit the use of props as they tend to be distracting.

9. When submitting the actual files:

   a. The file attachment should be in Quick Time, no larger than 25 MB. If using a PC, Windows Media or .wmv files work as well. If submitting multiple scenes in one file, Quick Time easily converts to smaller file sizes. DO NOT submit files larger than 50 MB's.

   b. If the audition has multiple scenes, edit and combine them all into one file for submission.

   c. Label your audition file(s) clearly and consistently, be it the audition scene, your headshot or your resume. Example:

   Audition Scene File Name:

   ActorsFirstName.ActorsLastName.CharacterName .AgencyAbbreviation.extension

   "Extenstion" means the type of file, such as .mov, .avi, .mp4, or .wmv. Translated, it looks something like this:

   Beverly.Leech.DrMarlowe.HsofRep.mp4
   Beverly.Leech.DrMarlowe.HsofRep.Resume
   Beverly.Leech.DrMarlowe.HsofRep.Headshot

10. DO NOT upload any audition video to any public site for any reason. You may accidentally divulge and spoil story arcs, plot points, and character development that the producing entity wants to keep private.

CHAPTER 5

AUDITIONS FOR THEATRE

Although I've made my living in the last several years in television, I began my career and worked for years on the stage. I also trained hard and received some of the best theatrical training directly from the late, great Stella Adler. I continue to work on stage any time the opportunity arises, as it's my first great love.

Many actors coming to Los Angeles are so focused on becoming film or television actors that they overlook the strength and integrity that stage work provides. One can get very spoiled and undisciplined with an on-set experience, but a theatrically trained actor knows that he gets only one chance a night to get it right and takes this skill and attitude to the set.

Because the Los Angeles pilot and episodic market is largely seasonal, I encourage every single actor out there to audition for stage, most especially during the hiatus and summer months. It keeps the seasoned professional fluid, and the unseasoned youngblood developing skills beyond all previous levels.

Although Los Angeles is not really wired for theatre rats like me, stage credits are still highly respected and often regarded as the sign of a real actor. My first union card, in fact, was with Actor's Equity Association (AEA), and many well-paying opportunities exist here in Los Angeles.

ACTORS EQUITY AUDITION POSTING

If you have aspirations for stage, one of the best sources of information for theatre auditions is Actor's Equity Association. You can access the best up-to-date information 24/7 online at actorsequity.org.

When you visit AEA's homepage, look for the icons near the headers to find a treasure trove of information. Up-to-date postings on theatre auditions can be found through the "Casting Call" icon. You'll find regional auditions throughout the country and under all types of contracts - from League of Resident Theatres (Lort A) to dinner theatre and casinos. You can also search by type of casting call (principal or chorus, as well as non-union principal and chorus.) Actor's Equity Association keeps track of new postings every week and also represents stage managers.

Additionally, under the "Document Library" icon, you'll find the standard contract agreements for each major city, regional market, and category of show; as well as protocol for professional conduct. Below is a sample of one such document of the code at an Equity Principle Audition Procedure for Los Angeles.

EQUITY PRINCIPAL AUDITION PROCEDURES – L.A.[3]

The following are the procedures for Principal Auditions required by Equity contract for Equity performers (EPAs.) Equity staff and monitors are responsible for fully enforcing this Code.

Questions, complaints and/or suggestions regarding this Code and its administration should be sent, in writing, to the Audition Department. They will be referred to the Auditions committee for further discussion. Your cooperation is very much appreciated!

1. An official monitor will only be present at official EPAs that are required by contract.

2. Monitors will report violations of Equity's "Safe and Sanitary" rules.

3. Monitors and Equity staff are not permitted to have any discussion regarding anyone who is auditioning, nor may they discuss any casting issues, with the employer's casting personnel.

4. You must have your paid-up membership card with you at the audition or written verification from the Membership Department of your paid membership status. Due to a high volume of activity, membership cannot be verified by telephone.

5. Monitors will sign performers only on the official EPA Sign Up Sheets.

6. The monitor will arrive one hour prior to the scheduled start of the call. The only official list of performers will be the one established by the monitor. Only those actually present with paid-up membership cards will be placed on the list. You will be required to show your membership card again prior to admission into the audition room.

---

3 *Reprinted with the permission of Actor's Equity Association.*

7. Should performers who are present before the start of the call choose to establish and honor an unofficial list/order among themselves, the Equity monitor will sign up those performers in the order in which they present themselves. This order must be established before the official start of the call. However, Equity and the Equity monitor can take no responsibility in organizing and/or coordinating any such unofficial list/order.

8. Day of Audition. Appointments will be scheduled only on the day of the audition in the following manner;

9. Six performers will be scheduled in twenty minute blocks of time. The length of each performer's audition will be at the discretion of the casting director, with a minimum of one minute given to each performer. Any time left over within the twenty minute block will be assigned to "alternates" (see below.)

10. You will choose a 20 minute time slot for the audition and be issued a white principal audition card with the time slot indicated on it. Time slots are available on a first come first served basis.

11. There is also an open-ended alternate list. This list will help to accommodate those who arrive after all time slots have been filled. The alternates will be "filtered" into the auditions as time permits. "Open-ended" means that you may sign the alternate sheet at any time. You could, for example, choose to be an alternate instead of choosing a specific time slot. Should you choose, however, to be on both lists, you must sign the first list and go to the rear of the line to sign another list.

12. You must arrive and check with the monitor ten minutes prior to your audition time slot (as calculated by the clock in the Audition Center, or by the monitor if the audition is in another

location.) If you are not present on time, an alternate will be given the appointment, time permitting. There can be no exceptions to this procedure.

13. If you are an alternate, you must be available when your name is called. If you are not present when your name is called, you will lose the alternate slot. Please understand that there is no guarantee that alternates will be seen.

14. If you miss your scheduled time or alternate slot, you are permitted to re-sign on the alternate list.

15. A time slot insures an audition during that 20 minute time period. If the audition process moves quickly, you may audition earlier than the scheduled time slots. However, your time slot will be honored, provided that you arrive 10 minutes before the scheduled time.

16. When there is a lunch break, the monitor will post a Lunch Time Information Sheet with the following: name of show; time of break; and time monitor will return.

17. Sign-in sheets will not be "carried over" to the next day.

18. At the conclusion of each day's auditions, the monitor will provide the casting personnel a list of the performers who signed up but were not seen, together with their pictures/resumes.

19. Audition centers are places of business. Food, pets, large packages, friends and/or relatives will not be permitted access. Noise levels should be kept to a minimum. Please also try to keep the waiting area neat and clean, as a courtesy to all others, and place trash in the proper receptacles. Smoking is not permitted in the audition area at any time.

20. After completing your audition, please leave the area quietly as a professional courtesy to the other performers who are still waiting. We ask that you always conduct yourselves as professionals. Should there be a problem or disturbance, however, please note that the Equity Council has affirmed the policy whereby, if necessary, anyone who creates a serious disturbance shall, at discretion of the staff, be removed from the audition area. Should you wish to report any infractions or suggest improvements in the administration of this Code, please do so by sending a signed letter to the Equity Audition Department. These procedures are developed around contractually bargained Agreements between Equity and Producers. Since each contract is negotiated separately, terms and conditions are never exactly the same in each contract. Therefore, please refer to the attached sheet to determine the specific EPI/A requirements of the contracts.

24-HOUR AUDITION INFORMATION
actorsequity.org/CastingCall
New York 877-AEA-1913 ext. 831
Chicago 877-AEA-1913 ext. 815
Los Angeles 877-AEA-1913 ext. 826
Orlando 877-AEA-1913 ext. 821
San Francisco 877-AEA-1913 ext. 836
Principal and Chorus Audition Procedures for New York and Los Angeles are available online at actorsequity.org

SAMPLE POSTING OF THEATRE PROTOCOL IN L.A.

The Center Theatre Group oversees productions on these three stages: The Mark Taper Forum, The Ahmanson Theatre, and the Kirk Douglas Theatre. For the purposes of teaching and comparison of regional protocol, below is a recent posting of the Mark Taper Forum's requests for their Equity General Auditions. Visit their website for any updates to the sample below. You can find parking instructions as well as the specific dates for the auditions. For more information on other employment opportunities with CTG, go to centertheatregroup.org.

MARK TAPER FORUM (CENTER THEATRE GROUP)

AEA REQUIRED AUDITIONS: Details for all AEA calls are given to Equity at least two weeks prior to the auditions.

EQUITY MONTHLY LOCAL OPEN CALLS

Center Theatre Group holds Equity general auditions on the first or second Monday of each month at the Music Center Annex. The Annex is located at 601 West Temple St. Doors open at 9:00 a.m. and we take the first 25 people who sign up. The sign-up is first come first served; no reservations will be taken. Auditions begin at 9:30 a.m. Sign-up ends at 9:30 a.m. You must be a member of AEA or EMC in good standing. [We do not see non-AEA/EMC actors on this day. Efforts to crash will not be entertained.]

For the audition you should prepare two contrasting 2 to 3 minute contemporary monologues. We prefer a piece from a published play performed without accent.

Please bring one stapled picture & resume.

Please note that if you have auditioned within the last six months we do not need to see you again and would appreciate your abstaining from attending so that we may get to know new people. Before coming to the audition you always should check here or at the AEA site to make sure the auditions have not been cancelled or rescheduled.

EQUITY PRINCIPAL AUDITIONS/EQUITY CHORUS CALLS (EPA/ECC)

We hold Equity Principal Auditions periodically – usually once a season in the Fall in Los Angeles and often in New York. Once the Equity general audition dates are announced, you can either make an appointment at the Equity office or come the day-of the audition. All things about these calls are monitored by Equity, and not CTG Casting. If you have questions – you need to contact Equity.

In the seasons when we are producing musicals or shows with music, CTG also holds separate required musical auditions - EPA and ECC's.

OPEN CALLS (NON-REQUIRED)

On occasion for select projects, we hold open calls for actors[4], musicians and other artists – please check back for notices.

---

[4] Prior to 2014, the Mark Taper/CTG posted this instruction for NON-EQUITY ACTORS: *"We are accepting pictures and resumes for all non-Equity actors. Please mail them with a cover letter to Center Theatre*

AUDITIONS (PROJECT SPECIFIC)

All auditions are by appointment/invitation only. Please see details in breakdowns and instructions on how to submit.

Please note our ability to hire those actors outside of LA is limited. Please respect when we request "LOCAL HIRE ONLY" submissions.

Production auditions are held throughout the season by invitation. We hold auditions often in New York, as well as other cities as needed.

OTHER AVENUES FOR PROFESSIONAL THEATRE in L.A.

More paying theatre for actors is available under a LORT contract at such venues as The Actor Gang, The Geffen, Laguna Playhouse, Pasadena Playhouse, Playwrights Arena, South Coast Repertory, Shakespeare Center, and a whole host of LOA and Guest Artists contracts at several theatres throughout California. You can find more listings on the Equity website, Backstage.com, and through your agent/breakdowns for opportunities in professional plays and musical theatre. If you have the chops, I heartily encourage you to balance your camera credits with stage experience. Theatre is the mark of endurance and artistry.

Group Casting, 601 West Temple Street, Los Angeles, CA 90012. When time permits, we hold general auditions by appointment for non-Equity actors." This statement is no longer posted to their website, so it is unclear at this time if they maintain this policy.

REGIONAL COMBINED THEATRE AUDITIONS

In addition to the AEA 'Casting Call' site, if you are looking for theatre outside of L.A., simply search with the keywords "2014 regional combined theatre auditions," or visit the Backstage.com listing and any other number of sites that host the information. Combined regionals bring several theatres to one location, allowing the actor to audition for all of them at the same time - kind of one-stop-shopping for both the actor and the producer. Redbird Studio has a rather clear explanation of the process below. [5]

Source: redbirdstudio.com/AWOL/combaud.html
"Looking for work in summer-stock productions, touring productions, Renaissance fairs, non-equity and equity theatres, Shakespeare festivals, theme parks, dinner theatre and outdoor dramas? Planning to enroll in a graduate level college theatre program? Want to audition for dozens of producers at one time? Want a rare opportunity to meet lots of producers and directors in the business? Make contacts? Get yourself known?

These regional combined auditions are a low-cost way to do exactly that. Every year, in February or March, each of these combined auditions are attended by dozens of producers who are looking for talented actors and actresses to perform in live summertime productions. Some also offer year-round positions in acting companies, school touring, apprentice and intern positions. Graduate school programs use many of these auditions to enroll students.

---

[5] *Reprinted with permission from Acting Workshop Online (AWOL) and Redbird Studio.*

Many of the organizations offer, for a small fee, a variety of workshops in addition to auditions. These workshops can be attended by those who audition and those who do not audition.

Send a self-addressed stamped envelope to the organizations that interest you, and request information about their auditions and an application. Because the auditions generally occur in February and March, write for information and applications in early December.

The regional auditions listed below are not for beginners new to the stage. They are for experienced, talented, skilled performers. Most (not all) require that you are at least 18 years old to apply and that you're available to work all summer long. Almost all are open to non-equity as well as equity performers. There are always many more applicants than audition spots available. APPLY EARLY! These are extremely competitive auditions. Applicants are screened, and many don't get in."

Examples of some of the opportunities posted are:

Atlanta Unified Auditions: atlantaperforms.biz
Boston Area Combined Stagesource Annual Auditions: stagesource.org
Florida Professional Theatres Association: fpta.net
League of Washington DC Area Theatres: lowt.org

Additional postings on this site include Midwest, New England Theatre Conference, Portland, Philadelphia, Ohio, Illinois, New Jersey Theatre Alliance, Southeastern Theatre Conference, and many, many more. There is a brief description of what each region requires for their combined theatre auditions, but a link to each is provided for more information.

"THE LEAGUES"
Interview with actress Samira Nikain

My experience is that regional, combined auditions are rigorous, not for the faint of heart, and I like to hear from other actors who have been through it, too. I find it reassuring that the "rules" are real, and I'm more vigilant and less tempted to fudge on my timing and preparation. Below is a lovely interview with one of my former protégés who received six or more callbacks from several acting companies at LOWT's combined regional auditions held in Washington D.C.

Tell me about your experience auditioning for the League Auditions ... Their requirements: time limits, types of audition monologues they were looking for.

The technical requirements: a monologue = 1½ to 2½ minutes and NO MORE ... THEY WILL STOP YOU. Contemporary or classical is fine. You may perform two contrasting monologues as long as they fit in the time allotted. You should be in comfortable clothing that allows them to see YOU the actor. No props. Something published ... no original works (although I didn't follow this rule ... I'll explain later.) If you choose to perform a song, you must perform it a cappella, and in the time allotted. No piano accompaniment is provided.

The requirements differ for each actor. If you are a first-timer (like me) then they prefer you to stay away from accents and even Shakespeare. The accents rule is because if this is your first Leagues audition they will be unsure if your accent is authentic or not. But of course actors will do what they want to do. Every year after your first audition you have more freedom as an actor to showcase your talent(s.) This audition is for professionals only ... you cannot be green, just starting out. You need to have either the foundation of a good school or professional credits.

How did you find out about them and how did you get an appointment?

My friend was in the costume department at The Folger Theatre, and told me about them years ago. Of course, with my plans for L.A., I never paid attention. Then I checked out their website at lowt.org and found that you could audition by belonging either to AEA or The Actor's Center (I believe L.A. has one also, but I am not sure if they are the same affiliation.)

So I joined the Actor's Center to be part of early registration. Equity and Actor's Center get to sign up first, then everyone else. And when you do sign up, everyone goes to an Open Call where you wait in line. It is two days of Open Calls from 10 a.m. to 7 p.m. Let's just say the line began at around 7 a.m.

You must bring (cannot remember the exact number) 56 to 70 headshots and resumes (stapled and completed.) You have to bring the exact number for all the theatre company: Casting Directors, Producers, Artistic Directors ... yada, yada, yada ... everyone who attends. No more, no less.

If anything is incomplete, you will not be allowed to sign up. Then you choose your audition date and time. You choose 30-minute increments, for example Monday 06/19 at 1:30 – 2 p.m. or Wednesday 06/21 at 4 – 4:30 p.m. The entire audition process takes over two weeks, and runs 3-4 days a week.

Where were they held?

Round House Theatre in Maryland, where they are held every year.

How long after auditioning did you have to wait before being contacted for a callback?

This varied based on theatre companies and their season schedules. I got three callbacks within one and a half weeks from the Smithsonian, Shakespeare Theatre Company, and the Studio Theatre. A month later, another call came from the Kennedy Center. Then I received two more calls in December from the Theatre Director at Georgetown University, who was putting together a reading for an upcoming playwright, and another from an Alexandria theatre company. So they varied based on the individual need and scheduling of each company. It's kind of like Hanukkah ... you get your gifts little by little.

Was the callback experience different from the open call, and how so?

The callback was more intimate. At the open call, you see a crowd of almost 100 people out there ... no faces ... but in the callbacks you meet the casting director of the theatre, perhaps a choreographer and director from the season's lineup etc. I did an initial callback for The Shakespeare Company (and this is where I performed Beatrice and Roxanne) and then they called me back again later for two more of their shows.

What was the process you actually went through on the day of the open call audition – signing in, waiting time, etc.?

You must arrive 30 minutes early or you will not be permitted in. They take you backstage of the theatre in groups of ten. One by one, each actor auditions. Once the person in front of you finishes their piece and walks offstage you must enter the stage. Time is important here! There is a board with all theatre and reps from those theatres posted. You can choose to copy them down or purchase the information packet for 10 dollars. I had a very nice pen and an exquisite notepad that I put to use!

Any stories or observations you had about actors behaving badly, or winning stories about the ones that seemed to succeed in the process?

I found a tremendous range of actors: many ages, races, etc. Many of them knew each other before and therefore were calm and composed ... on the outside anyway. I found every actor to be respectful of each other and gave each other space to stay focused. There were actors doing stretches, some were doing vocal warm-ups. A few actors, when they found out I was new, decided to give me their negative opinions. One guy said, "They won't call you the first year you audition. They make you sweat ... took them four years to finally give me a callback."

I heard his audition and it was performed well. I am lucky that I am ethnic; I believe that actually gave me the upper hand and I was fortunate enough to get callbacks. Oddly, there was a more professional vibe at the Leagues than at the callbacks. At one of my callbacks for the Studio Theatre there were a bunch of actors joking around and not staying focused. There are also a lot of pretty faces. When we went in to the audition (group audition – 10 at a time) I found only three people who weren't "acting;" the rest looked like actor-American Idol rejects.

If you had any advice to actors based on this experience, what would it be?

Be prepared. Do the work. Relax ... don't look at any audition, especially one like this, as your final hope. We are actors – we survive. Be on time. Don't choose a piece because it's good ... make sure it's good for you! I always feel like an audition is my wedding day. I don't want to wear just any dress. I want my dress ... the one that is going to make me look fabulous and stand out. If a monologue isn't a wedding dress then I start over.

Again ... be prepared.

URTA: UNIVERSITY RESIDENT THEATRE ASSOCIATION

URTA.com

If you haven't decided to go pro, and are considering an academic route, I would heartily encourage you to consider the URTA auditions. Graduate school is one of several good options when pursuing training and a career in any field of the performing arts. Ty Burrell, star of *Modern Family,* came out of an URTA school and gained an agent from participating in post-graduate auditions. URTA allows you to audition for many university theatre programs at one time, instead of applying and traveling to each campus separately. URTA's audition standards closely mirror professional protocol, and their reputation is bolstered with award-winning theatre companies.

I've found that URTA's audition process described in their manual, *NUIA Handbook (section for acting auditions)*, exactly reflects the experience I've had at every professional audition for regional theatre and Broadway. You would be wise to study the entire handbook and take its suggestions and structure to heart – it will serve you well in every circumstance.

THE BENEFITS OF URTA AND THE RECRUITMENT PROCESS:

Each year the University/Resident Theatre Association holds National Unified Auditions/Interviews (often referred to as "The URTAs") for outstanding graduating and advanced theatre students. Older candidates, and candidates who majored in fields other than theatre or drama, make up a sizable portion of the applicant pool. Talented acting, design, directing, stage management, technical, and theatre management candidates are offered the opportunity to compete for numerous positions with graduate schools and partnered theatre companies. Most positions offered through URTA receive financial assistance.

Since 1970, the URTAs have provided candidates the chance to obtain positions in graduate (MFA) training. Acting candidates audition before representatives from among the many member graduate programs and partnered professional theatre companies associated with URTA. A second set of Satellite Auditions is available for the interested Actor, where non-member guest programs participate, often including several international schools. Designers present their portfolios for review by representatives from the premiere graduate design and technology programs in the country, along with guest attendance by summer companies looking to employee crew and staff for their seasons. Directors, stage managers, and theatre managers also have the chance to interview with faculty recruiters from URTA member institutions and guest participants. Efficient, effective, and financially sensible, The URTAs are an important option to consider by those looking for professional graduate training.

URTA videos are available for review at urta.com. Their handbook, *URTA Handbook for NUAI Candidates, 2014* is next, and can also be found online at urta.com through their "download center."[6]

---

[6] *Re-printed with permission of the University/Resident Theatre Association (URTA) April, 2012. The NUIA Handbook is revised and published annually by URTA. No other use or exploitation of this material is permitted without prior agreement with URTA.*

URTA

University/Resident Theatre Association

Handbook for NUAI Candidates
2014 GUIDELINE FOR ACTORS

Now Available! URTA's videos about the
Audition/Interview Process and Design/Technical
Portfolio Reviews – visit urta.com to watch them free

University/Resident Theatre Association, Inc.
1560 Broadway, Suite 1103, New York, NY 10036
(212)221-1130 Fax: (212)869-2752
Audition Hotline (520)760-2434
www.URTA.com
email: auditions@urta.com

GENERAL INFORMATION
The primary ingredient of any successful audition is
centered in truthful and imaginative acting, employing
skills and techniques that are very similar to those used
for playing a role in a production. What stands out as a
major difference is that in a play, the actor is part of a
production, but in an audition, the actor is the
production. While each audition needs to be fully
analyzed, passionate, and well-rehearsed, you still need
to make sure that you show the Recruiters who you are,
what you are capable of (*at this point in your training*),

and why they should consider you for their specific program.

Ask yourself the basic questions about your audition piece: 1. To whom am I talking? 2. What I am trying to get them to do, or how am I changing their behavior? Then concentrate your energies not on showing yourself to the audience, but on getting the person to whom you are speaking to change in the way you want. If you focus on changing the other person, then the audience gets to see more of you. Thus a fine audition is a revelation of "Self," not a slick impersonation. Inappropriate selection of material and poor presentation techniques are the two most common faults in general auditions. Both areas demand objectivity, which is why an audition coach is strongly suggested.

There are many excellent books on the audition process. Three classics are:

Shurtleff, Michael and Fosse, Bob. <u>Audition: Everything An Actor Needs to Know to Get the Part</u>. Walker & Company, 2003.

Cohen, Robert. <u>Acting Professionally</u>. McGraw-Hill Humanities, 5th ed., 1997.

Ellis, Roger. <u>The Complete Audition Book for Young Actors</u>. Meriwether Publishing, 2003.

<u>AUDITION FORMAT</u>

1. **Acting Auditions are two minutes in length**. This includes your introduction and transitions, but does not include your entrance and exit into the room. You are free to do whatever you wish in the two minutes, but our suggestion is two contrasting monologues. If you choose to do two monologues, they do not have to be the same length. Again, the choice is yours, but remember to find pieces that are active;

where you need to change something in the other person.

2. When you enter the audition space, the stage manager announces your name and you walk onto the stage. Set the table and chair if you are using them; then you may acknowledge the auditors with a "Good morning" or "Hello" and a repeat of your name. Then do your introduction, i.e. "My first piece is (<u>Character's Name</u>) from (<u>Play Title</u>)." Do not surprise the auditors without an introduction, no matter how clever or dramatic. If you do, auditors may spend the first few moments reflecting on your lack of introduction rather than your audition.

3. Timing **begins** when you introduce your audition. You may introduce both pieces if you are doing two, or individually before each piece. If you introduce them both at the start, it is VITAL that you take the transition time between the two pieces. Think of organizing your audition as a one-act play containing major "beats" or "units of action:"

1. Your entrance and greeting.
2. Introduction of Selection #1.
3. Transition from yourself to character #1.
4. Presentation of your first selection.
5. Transition from character #1 back to yourself.
6. Introduction of selection #2.
7. Transition from yourself to character #2.
8. Presentation of your second selection.
9. Transition from character #2 back into yourself.
10. Thank you and exit.

4. Consider, play and rehearse each beat carefully. Your entrance, transitions, thank you and exit are most definitely part of your audition, though the entrance and exit is not included in your timing.

5. Don't rush transitions. For this audition, how you "shift gears" from one part of the audition to the next is important. If ignored, auditions tend to blur into two general minutes of non-specific "performing." Transitions give you a chance to catch your breath under the potentially nerve-wracking circumstances of an audition. Rushing from an introduction into a monologue or from one piece to another without ever shifting gears destroys the dramatic illusion, so, please, don't forget to breathe.

6. Never emotionalize, editorialize, or apologize for your audition. What may have gone wrong for you might have gone unnoticed by the auditors. Your audition begins with your entrance so maintain a confident, positive persona. Don't be nasty if the stage manager mangles your name ... a smile and a gentle correction is much better. Similarly if you are stopped, don't huff and puff and stomp off stage. Again, the smile, and a nice thank you is the wisest choice.

7. Don't be thrown or concerned by lack of response from the Recruiters. They tend to remain neutral or slightly detached during auditions in order to maintain their objectivity. Lack of response does not mean they don't like what you're doing.

AUDITION MATERIAL SELECTION

1. Never attempt an audition monologue without reading the entire play and understanding your character in the context of the play. <u>Pay close attention to this point if you search for material from monologue collections!</u> Material from these collections can be "overdone."

2. If you do two selections, they should be CONTRASTING. The standard choice is a contemporary prose piece together with a period verse piece. However "Contrast" does not ONLY mean "Shakespeare and

Sarah Ruhl." It can be demonstrated through type of character and material. Consider contrasting a dramatic piece with a comedic one; or prosaic/poetic; urban/rural; etc. Look for selections with contrasts in mood, intention, rhythm, emotional level, content, etc. Be aware that if you do NOT do a classical piece in your audition, <u>you may be asked for one if you get Callbacks</u>. Keep in mind that Shakespeare is not the only classical playwright. Strong audition pieces can be found in the Greek plays, as well as Shakespeare's contemporaries and those of the Restoration.

3. Avoid climactic material that requires great depth or intensity of emotion. There is not enough time to achieve these emotional peaks effectively and honestly. On the other hand, beware of dull and passive pieces which dwell on character or plot exposition. Also, do not choose pieces that are stories or comic routines without a connection to the person to whom you are speaking.

4. Selection(s) should be self-explanatory with a clear beginning, middle and end. Two or more speeches may be combined to form a monologue, as long as connections are smooth and logical. Test the clarity of your piece by reading it to someone unfamiliar with the play. If there is confusion regarding the Who, What, Why, When or Where of the piece, it should be eliminated.

5. Avoid one-person show material. The Recruiters want to see YOU, not your interpretation of a celebrity. We also do not recommend using original material. While you may be the next great American playwright, recruiters may be caught off guard, and spend the first minute of your audition trying to figure out where the piece came from.

6. Sexually explicit or extremely offensive material may work against you. While eccentric selections may be attention-getters, remember that your material is a

reflection of your taste. Recruiters are not fuddy duddy prudes, but given the brief time you have on stage, it is best to leave a positive impression. Likewise, *good* writing will always serve you better than mediocre writing. You know the expression, "you are what you eat?" Here, "you are what you present." Your material choice counts a great deal, so choose the best pieces you can!

7. It is wise to brush up on any extra selections you may have in your audition repertoire as some schools will give you the opportunity to present additional pieces during the Callbacks.

PREPARING YOUR AUDITION

1. Reminder: audition time is <u>TWO MINUTES</u>. Set up a schedule with your coach if you are using one (*we suggest using a coach who is familiar with URTA auditions*), allowing time to review, select and edit pieces and rehearse thoroughly. Discuss your interpretation with your coach to be sure you have a solid understanding of given circumstances, character, intentions, obstacles, and relationships for each of your characters. Present "dry runs" in a variety of spaces, in front of two or three faculty members or fellow students, both for critical feedback and for practice in auditioning for a group of people. You will most likely not know the dimensions or type of room you are auditioning in until you arrive, so it is best to be prepared for anything!

2. Do not direct your focus directly to one of the recruiters. The recruiter may not be able to evaluate you impartially if you ask them to come into the world of your monologue. Keep your imaginary partner on stage with you (*downstage, please*). Playing towards an empty seat in the audience, or in the direction of the light booth are stronger choices for the purposes of this

audition. Avoid putting the other character on the floor to keep your face up.

3. Stage your audition simply, utilizing a minimum of space -- preferably within a radius of 5-10 feet. This does not mean to say you must "restrict" your movements, however. Stage yourself 3/4 to full front, since your best side is the one with your face! A table and chair are available, but you don't have to use them. No props, unless it is something you might normally wear or carry, such as glasses, a handkerchief, a letter in your pocket, a scarf, a jacket, etc. The focus should be on you, not on your set design.

4. Be confident that your total presentation, **including introduction and transitions**, comes in under two minutes. You do not want to worry about being cut off, so eliminate this concern now. "Talking fast" or rushing your transitions will NOT give you more time. Michael Shurtleff, the dean of audition training, insists, "no audition is ever too short." Timing is enforced and if you run over, you will be asked to stop.

SINGING AUDITIONS (Optional)

1. If you are a strong singer, you may have an additional 16 bars not to exceed 30 seconds. None of our MFA programs recruit for Musical Theatre specifically. A bad song after a good acting audition can leave doubt in the recruiters' minds. We discourage singing unless you are certain you have a strong voice, or that your song communicates something important about you as an actor. Regardless, ask yourself the same questions about your song as you do with your monologues. At URTA, you must both sing and act your song well.

2. Bring a battery operated media player for accompaniment (*and don't forget to charge it or bring batteries as an outlet will not be provided*). A cappella

singing is not permitted. Cue up your selection <u>before</u> entering the audition room. Place the player at the foot of the stage or on the table, *facing towards you,* so that you can hear the accompaniment and the Recruiters can hear you. You may not accompany yourself on guitar, or anything else

3. Favor upbeat show tunes in your selection.

4. This is an opportunity to demonstrate that you are an accomplished actor who can also sing, and is not an audition for a musical. The 30 seconds are **in addition to** your 2 minutes of acting. Timing is enforced and begins when you start to sing. And no, you can't sing for 2 minutes and do a 30 second audition, so don't even ask!

<u>AUDITION SPACE</u>

1. You will have a chance to preview the audition space, test the acoustics and walk the stage before or during the morning orientation. If you arrive late, you may miss this opportunity. Be aware of where you are going, what door you use to get out, where the chair is, if you plan to use it, find your light, etc.

2. Relate to your environment throughout the audition. Establishing an environment (*indoor, outdoor, familiar, unfamiliar, etc.*) and attitudinal relationships to other characters are two of the most useful, and most frequently overlooked, acting tools in an audition.

<u>WHAT TO BRING/WHAT TO WEAR</u>

1. Clean, neat, comfortable and relatively conservative clothing is usually the best choice. Do not try to "costume" yourself, but avoid apparel that contradicts your character (*i.e. royalty in running shoes, Noel Coward in tee-shirts, etc.*). Make sure your hair is off your face. Dangling, jangling jewelry is distracting. Do you really need to assert your individuality by

wearing your tongue stud? Generally a button down shirt or sport coat with nice slacks for men; a blouse and skirt/slacks, or a dress for women, works well.

2. You do not need to bring them to the Audition, but if you receive any Callbacks, you may need your picture/resume (*stapled back to back*) and <u>photocopies</u> of your transcripts. We suggest 5 - 10 of each. Insure that your resume's contact information is accurate, particularly phone and email.

3. Yes, photocopies of your scholastic transcripts are fine. You may or may not need these if you receive Callback/Interviews. Please do not mail them to the URTA office.

WHEN YOU ARRIVE

1. Orientation is mandatory on the morning of your URTA Audition. Your email will tell you what TIME your Orientation is. There may be more than one Orientation each day, so please attend the one indicated in your email. Plan to arrive early enough to check in <u>before</u> Orientation begins.

2. At the Orientation, you will meet the stage manager and see the audition space. You will be told what time, later that same day, results will be distributed. After Orientation, you may leave, but plan to be back **at least** 30 – 40 minutes before your scheduled audition time as we sometimes pick up time.

3. You will do your audition for the recruiters from URTA institutions and our guest participants. You are free to leave when you are done, but remember to come back later THAT SAME DAY at the appointed time.

4. When you come back that afternoon, you will receive a sheet that lists any Callbacks you may have received. URTA has scheduled these for you, and they begin immediately. There is no way to determine how late these may go, or how many Callbacks you could

receive. After the Callbacks, if you get any, your obligation to the URTA Auditions is complete, and you may leave, unless you are also participating in the Satellite Auditions (*Please see separate section*).

PREPARING FOR A CALLBACK/INTERVIEW

1. Research programs in advance using the enclosed Directory, and the vast resources available on the internet. Links to URTA members are on our website. Do not wait until the interview to find out what type of training each program offers. Take the responsibility and be informed.

2. Arrange practice sessions with someone such as your coach acting as a recruiter. Be prepared to answer questions regarding your training needs and career goals. Be specific - the statement, "I want to be a working actor" is too general. This is the time to be yourself. Recruiters are not just interested in your talent or potential but WHO you are as a person. Remember that you are both looking at each other with the idea that you will spend a great deal of time together over the next several years.

3. Each Callback/Interview is slightly different. Some recruiters just want to find out more about you, some will want to discuss their programs. Others may ask you to "work" on a piece, maybe something you did in your audition or maybe something else. You could be alone, or in a group of other actors. We suggest that you be open to any adjustment or situation that may be thrown your way.

4. Each Interview lasts 15 minutes with 5-minute transit time in between. Running around the hotel can be tiring, so be prepared. Bring a snack, some water, some breath mints, a hairbrush, so you can go into each interview looking your best. Don't forget headshots, resumes and transcripts.

SATELLITE AUDITIONS

When you sign up to do the **URTA Auditions**, you are applying to audition for our member schools and Guest Participants who are pursuing URTA membership. The **Satellite Auditions** are a separate, optional event in New York and Chicago, and are attended by Guest Participants who are not pursuing membership in URTA. In San Francisco, the Satellite Recruiters attend the URTA Auditions so a separate audition is not necessary.

    1. Candidate must be signed up for the URTA Auditions in order to be eligible to attend the Satellite Auditions too. The option to sign up for the Satellite Auditions was on the original application, but registered Candidates may add it on our web site, and when you arrive. There is an additional fee for the Satellite Audition, and space is limited.

    2. The Satellite Audition will take place on the day AFTER your URTA Audition - for example if your URTA Audition is on Monday, your Satellite Audition will be on Tuesday. It will be in a different location than the URTA Audition. You will receive your time by email. Unfortunately, you cannot do the URTA Audition AND the Satellite Audition on the same day.

SATELLITE AUDITIONS FORMAT

    1. Mandatory Orientation for Satellite Auditions is at 9:30am on the day of your Satellite Audition. Check in before Orientation begins. You will meet the stage manager and see the audition space. You do not need picture/resume at this time. After Orientation, you may leave the area, but return **at least** 30 – 40 minutes before your scheduled audition time.

2. The Satellite Audition works the same as the URTA Audition - your name is announced by the stage manager, and timing begins when you introduce your piece. Candidate has two minutes to present the same audition material as prepared for the URTA Audition, or something else. There will also be the additional 30 seconds/16 bars to sing.

3. You can leave when you are done, but be sure to come back at the appointed time to review the callback sheets. If a program requests to see you, you will sign up right there for an appointment later that same day. There is no way to determine how late these may go, or how many Callbacks you could receive, if any. These callbacks are not controlled or scheduled by URTA.

BEFORE YOU LEAVE FOR YOUR AUDITION

- Does your audition consistently fall within the time limits, including transitions and the introduction?

- Have you performed the audition to an audience, in a variety of spaces?

- Do you enjoy performing these pieces? Does your audience like them?

- Is there a live, urgent objective for each piece?

- Do the pieces allow you to reveal **yourself**, rather than an impersonation?

FINAL NOTES

1. If you have an online resume or web site, and would like to make that available to the recruiters, please send it to auditions@urta.com by December 31st.

2. An audition is an *opportunity*, not a contest to be won or lost. Recruiters know there is no way to demonstrate all your talents, skills, and experience in a

single two-minute audition, so don't try! This is simply a brief introduction to your talent, personality and basic performance skills. Most of the Recruiters are actors themselves, and have been in your shoes, and appreciate how artificial and intense auditioning can be. Above all, they are on your side and are rooting for you. So, don't put any more pressure on yourself than necessary. Relax and do your best. You can't ask any more of yourself.

3. Re-read the application instructions, paying particular attention to the information pertaining to actors. Re-read the letter at the beginning of this document, and the emails sent by URTA, review the site sheet, check out the FAQ page and watch the video on the web page, and **then** read this Handbook again. It is 100% your responsibility to know what is going on and to understand the process. The URTA process can be exhausting, so keep that in mind when planning travel and scheduling other auditions.

4. If you signed up to do both the URTA Auditions and the Satellite Auditions, you must attend the orientation for each, on the day assigned. If you receive callbacks from the URTA Auditions, they are scheduled THE SAME DAY as your URTA Audition. Callbacks for the Satellite Auditions are held on the day of your Satellite Audition.

5. Break a Leg!

PLEASE READ EVERYTHING CAREFULLY. Read the FAQs on the website and watch the helpful videos about the audition/interview process on their website (www.urta.com). Additional questions not addressed in the Guidelines or on the website FAQ page, can be emailed to Sara Falconer, Director of Membership

Services at <u>auditions@urta.com</u>. You may also call
(520) 760-2434 during office hours 12 – 4pm Eastern
Standard Time.

CHAPTER 6

REPRESENTATION: AGENTS AND MANAGERS

TAKING A MEETING

THE AGENCY /MANAGER INTERVIEW

Taking a meeting is just as important as knowing how to act. Not every agency meeting is run the same way, but there are common elements that you can anticipate. Think about possible topics and practice your responses so you feel ready and confident. You don't need canned answers, but you do need mental preparation and flexibility. Spend some time in self-examination about your "type," and review your resume and online pages to look for any credit, skills, or people that they might bring up as talking points during the meeting.

One good meeting alone does not ensure an agency contract. Depending on the size of the company, it is often a series of meetings. The first one is with the primary, a "point man," one who has expressed interest and wants to get to know you better. Many times, getting signed requires that all the agents in the company are unanimous in interest and enthusiasm, so a second meeting may be scheduled for you to meet everyone. The suggestions below are good, basic tips to preparing for a meeting.

BEFORE THE MEETING

- Learn something about the agency. Check their credits and background by doing a little research. Review their websites and their client list on IMDb Pro. Click on the credits of their top clients and see what kind of projects they booked; this reflects the strength of an agent's relationships in the industry, and also indicates whether their projects are in line with your career plan. Note: just because the firm is small or new doesn't mean they're weak. Agents and managers who were once with large and powerful firms often leave and start their own companies. With that kind of background, they should have established solid contacts and negotiating skills.

- Be on time – in fact be a few minutes early. Reschedule if you are sick and contagious – they'll appreciate the respect.

- Bring two or three headshots and resumes, and a demo reel (or links) if you have one especially if you have film and television on your resume.

- Be well-groomed in "upscale casual" or attractive business attire – something you feel really good in. Jeans are fine as long as they're clean and dressed up with a great jacket and nice shoes. Never walk in looking like a starving actor, or as if you've just come from the gym.

DURING THE MEETING

BE YOURSELF, be positive, and add some charm and good manners. Put another way: Leave your bags at the stage door. Those bags are your personal problems. Don't bring your divorce, rehab, surgery, bankruptcy, or car trouble into the room with you. Save that for therapy. Also, if you're moving on from another agency, do not talk about what's wrong with your career or bash another agent or casting director – it might get repeated and karma's a bitch. Instead, anticipate negativity and phrase every response with a benign but positive spin, then change the subject. Using this subtle but necessary avoidance technique will keep the meeting clean – bitterness taints everything, including their first impression of you.

KEEP AN EASY SENSE OF HUMOR, and in a free-form way, be able to talk about both the personal and business side of yourself: your hobbies and social activities; how you see yourself in terms of type, shows, and genre; your efforts and career so far; your training and range of abilities; strong desires and accomplishments; and which sacrifices you're prepared to make. For instance, potential agents were concerned that I wouldn't work as often or that I might turn down work when I married and had a child – they were wrong. In fact, I booked more often and simply traveled with my daughter and a set nanny.

RELAX, if you're worried about being a lump on the couch and fielding questions. Sometimes the art of conversation is to get them to talk about themselves. A photo, piece of art, or collectible you see in the office can be a fun, casual, and easy start to a conversation. You can also take the temperature of the room when you walk in – if they're effervescent and jovial, the conversation should be rather easy to roll out. If they seem shy or tense, or in a bad mood, remember it's not personal – simply keep it light and professional and maintain your own sense of grace and charm. You might just be the breath of fresh air they need today. If they're ballbusting and gruff, don't get defensive and rattle your saber. A good sense of humor will keep you flexible and sharp.

CAN YOU ANSWER THE HARD QUESTION?

Besides potential earning power, the agent is interested in actors with a realistic sense of self, clarity, and a plan. Agents will often ask hard questions like these:

"How do you see yourself?" This means do you know your "type" in terms of roles, age range, film genres, or type of stage work. Be able to frame your look and abilities using other actors and projects currently on the market.

"What do you see yourself doing or accomplishing in one year?" What kind of roles can you book now, and reasonably upgrade in a short time?

"What do you see yourself doing or accomplishing in five years?" This is the long game, and it's about your potential for expansion into bigger contracts and types of work. It encompasses the TV/Film projects for which you'd be a good fit, or film or TV directors, TV show

runners, and writers you'd like to work with. You can add other interests such as producing, directing, writing, or stand-up comedy to your list if you're gifted or experienced in any of those areas.

THE WEAK ANSWER to the hard question:

- *"I don't know."* A balking, awkward silence. *"Uhmmmmmm ... (laugh)"*

- *"Be famous." "Win an Academy Award."* They'll just wince. It's a dream with fuzzy outlines, not a specific goal with immediate do-ables toward building a career.

- *"Go back to school and finish my degree."* This indicates you won't be in town or available to work. The industry isn't a hobby or a tryout – serious actors are ready to work.

- *"Get an agent so he can get me a job."* This isn't funny. It's uninformed sarcasm. Agents get you appointments; it's up to you to get the job.

QUESTIONS YOU CAN ASK

Remember this is a give-and-take conversation between two parties, a mutual discussion. Don't forget that agents work for you, not the other way around, and there should be a friendly balance of mutual expectations. The personable conversation usually seems to go well, but many actors don't know that they can ask business questions, too. Doing background homework on the agency beforehand will also answer many of these questions so you won't have to ask.

How do you see me? It's a fair question and a great discussion point. The answer might be different from how you see yourself or the goals you've set.

How many clients do you represent? And/or, *How many men (or women) do you have in my category and type?* Then, mentally calculate whether they have enough manpower and employees to keep things balanced – and still have time and energy for you.

Do you have an East Coast branch or work in tandem with any agencies/managers there?

Do you submit for theatre? You'd be surprised how many do not. If not, and you want to play the boards, ask if they have any problem with your self-submitting for those projects. Many agents are worried that doing stage work will make you unavailable for more lucrative contracts in TV/Film. There is a solution. Equity projects often have understudies for their shows and their contracts provide outs for occasions in which you book TV/Film in the middle of the run. In Equity Waiver, an understudy can be negotiated before you accept the role. You shouldn't ever feel obligated to pass up a paying gig for an unpaid waiver role.

Which casting directors do you regularly speak with? For both managers and agents, feel free to find out what their strengths are in terms of shows, and with which casting directors they have a good rapport. Many agents split a casting list amongst the other agents, so you could ask which casting people their desk covers. Managers usually work alone and don't split a list. This is a good discussion point within a first meeting and should lend you some insight about the agent.

If the meeting feels light and breezy, feel free to ask more personable questions such as, *What's your favorite or most memorable story about a client booking? Or What's the best part about being an agent?*

Don't volunteer the information, but if they ask, it's okay to talk about any other agencies you've taken meetings with recently. Agents are usually quite curious and it may spark a little healthy competition to get you signed. But don't lie about it or name drop if it's not really true – they'll smell it. Or they'll pick up the phone and call the name you just volleyed – you never know who their friends are.

If this is your first agent and you don't have a reel, offer to do an audition monologue on the spot. Others will ask you to come back within the next couple of days or weeks with a scene..

Don't wear out your welcome. Sense when to quit talking and leave gracefully. A short meeting is not an indication that it didn't go well. Interviews can last anywhere from 20 minutes up to an hour. When you leave, leave with confidence and a good handshake. Don't ask if they're signing you, or linger awkwardly, hedging for an answer about when they'll be in touch. Just leave – it's called a clean exit. They'll let you know, believe me.

You have the right to walk away from any situation in which you feel forced or your gut instincts are telling you to slow down. If you sense you're in a bad situation, just quickly and gracefully end the meeting, take any paperwork offered and follow up later (if you choose.)

After the meeting, it's appropriate to send a brief and sincere thank-you note. Then, save your mental health by moving on and arranging the next interview with another agent.

WHEN AUDITIONS ARE PART OF THE INTERVIEW

Some commercial agency interviews ask you to cold read copy that they provide. You'll have about five to fifteen minutes to prepare. And theatrical agents and managers sometimes ask potential new clients to prepare either monologues or scenes for the meeting, especially if the actor is young or doesn't have a reel. For those, here are some guidelines for you to follow:

- Use only well-rehearsed material, not cold material (last-minute, with just a few hours or days of preparation.) Being well-prepared will give you confidence and spontaneity with the material. My personal preference is to rehearse two to four weeks in advance, with daily practice.

- Time your monologues and don't let them exceed one minute each. They'll be making decisions within the first 20 to 30 seconds. If they ask for a scene instead, a timing of two to four minutes is enough; any longer than that will have them fidgeting.

- Within that time limit, your material still must have a strong narrative (storyline) that is easy to follow, with a dynamic beginning and a strong ending. It's even better if your material has a good reveal or surprise buried in there.

- Choose material that you're cast-able in *today* and according to your type in age and personality. If it is for a casting, choose material that is close to the style and genre of their show.

- Perform your material fully, using filmic energy for camera, as a finished performance. Do it with honesty, and with your sense of largeness coming from an "inner size." For film and television agents, this ability is more appreciated than the high physicality needed for a stage audition.

- Don't choose a bag of tricks. Material that depends on props is a very special level of hell for the actor who isn't masterful with them. Props can enhance your acting by adding a touch of realism, but they can kill your efforts if they fail to work. If you use props, make sure they're simple and effortless to handle – like a watch, a pen, or a necktie. My best advice is to not use them at all.

- Do not choose iconic roles or material associated with a famous actor. They can't help but think about Robert Downey Jr. or Julia Roberts and miss the unique gifts and wonder that you have to offer. Cuttings from literature, one-acts, or ten-minute plays such as those published by Actors Theatre of Louisville often have great material that casting wouldn't have seen. Well-written television and independent films are also a good source, as are big films released five or more years ago that have the buffer of time between you and the role.

- I prepare myself both seated and standing as I never know what will be available to me in the room. You should minimize the space used in an office setting.

- Do not deliver your monologue straight to the agent as if they are the other character. Take your moment before to ground yourself in the character and scene, then focus to the left or right of their shoulder, or just above the top of their head if you're standing. Make that space your imaginary character.

- Even though you're well-rehearsed, try not to plan every moment and activity. It needs to look fluid, as if you're doing it for the first time.

- This is your time, so make it yours and let it rip. "Take the room," my mentor used to say.

- Love your work and invest in the moment. It's the best way to keep your nerves at bay.

- When finished, do not apologize for anything, and don't comment with a grimace on your performance. You see, in addition to talent, they're also assessing your level of confidence. If you fall apart in a meeting, you'll surely fall apart on a set where the stakes are higher. Simply return to your regular self and let the interview continue.

CHECKLIST FOR THE INTERVIEW

A. MATERIALS AND PRESENTATION

1. Enter with confidence and a good handshake. Photos and resume?

2. Dressed for success?

3. If film work indicated, demo?

B. PERSONAL INTERVIEW SKILLS
"Tell me about yourself." Brief background, interests, things you've been doing lately.

1. Best self?

2. At ease (physical tension)?

3. Positive spin on topics?

4. Freely engage agent in questions, not just answering them?

5. Able to improvise or give impromptu performances when asked?

6. Able to discuss credits/skills with ease and grace?

C. BUSINESS INTERVIEW SEGUE
Review Chapter 1 on "Goals" and Chapter 3 on "Type." These will help you shape your answers. Can you answer the hard questions?

1. "How do you see yourself"?

2. Type/roles/age range/genres within Film/TV or comedy/drama

3. Ready and flexible with the answer to Question 5? Or did you balk?

4. The One Year question: THE PLAN you have right now to work toward your goals.

5. The Five Year question: Regular working actor in the areas of _____.

D. CLOSING THE DEAL with your talent:
Audition monologue or scene: TV/Film preferred. Stage material is still appropriate if delivered with filmic energy. Lead with your strong suit. Have a second monologue ready in a contrasting style.

1. Appropriate material: Are you castable in it today?

2. Execution – energy and eyelines? Natural segues between yourself and the material?

3. Preparation – sufficiently rehearsed?

E. EXIT with confidence and a handshake. They'll determine a follow-up; don't linger.

DIFFERENCES BETWEEN AN AGENT AND A MANAGER

When seeking representation, you want someone that "gets" you, is enthusiastic and assertive in working for you, has strong industry connections, and can negotiate good deals on your behalf. Your first priority is to get an agent, a good agent. If you cannot get an agent, then a good, hard-working manager can be the next best thing. Managers often work in tandem with an agent (or an entertainment attorney) to bolster all efforts in furthering your career. Some actors prefer to have both because they like the "team," and other actors run with the idea that "if you have a good agent, you don't need a manager." Ultimately, it's your decision, but you should always do some homework to make informed decisions before you sign a contract with anyone.

Technically and ethically, Agents and Managers work for you, but it's a respectful collaboration of effort – both the actor and the rep work with and for each other. Agents and managers are similar in function but have some differences that should be clarified and addressed. Here are the broad strokes:

1. Both agents and managers are able to submit you on projects and pitch you to casting directors, producers, and directors. An agent's job is to get you auditions, but be clear – they get the appointment, and it's up to *you* get the job. Although they can provide counsel on your career path, they're often very busy. Managers normally have a smaller client list and can give you more personalized attention toward follow-ups with casting. They also oversee areas that are not within the agency's purview, such as personal appearances, networking, publicity, and marketing – and can offer more time in developing a plan for your career path.

2. Agents normally represent you in a specific field and medium (e.g. just commercials, or just theatrical; sometimes "across the board" but not often.) Managers usually ask for across the board representation, but don't assume that they will submit you across the board. Some managers handle TV/Film, but not commercials (or vice versa), yet will expect to receive commissions on all projects regardless of their direct efforts toward that booking. That's just the way it is. However, you're not completely tied to that arrangement. You always have the option of negotiating different terms.

3. Agents normally take 10 percent in commissions. Managers commonly take 15 percent. Never pay

and agent or manager up front to represent you. Their commission comes out of your payroll check from the work you book.

4. An agent must be licensed by their State, and must meet certain legal requirements in order to be licensed. A manager does not need a license in order to go into business – they just need a client who's willing to sign a contract. You can check for Talent Agency Licenses in California at www.dir.ca.gov/dlse/DLSE-Databases.htm, then scroll down to "Talent Agency License Database" to verify an agency license.

5. Since agencies are regulated by the state labor board, they must adhere to certain policies, duties, and definitions. The labor board gives agents the right to legally negotiate contracts on your behalf. Managers are not regulated or legally recognized as an occupation under California law, therefore they're technically not able to negotiate contracts. If you sign an agreement with a manager giving them permission to do so, there are some narrow margins of definition and protections within the statutes.

In California, the legal definition of a Talent Agent/Agency: *1700.4. (a) "a person or corporation who engages in the occupation of procuring, offering, promising, or attempting to procure employment or engagements for an artist or artists, except that the activities of procuring, offering, or promising to procure recording contracts for an artist or artists shall not of itself subject a person or corporation to regulation and licensing under this chapter. Talent agencies may, in addition, counsel or direct artists in the development of their professional careers."*

Because management isn't recognized as an occupation, you won't find a legal state definition for them. However, the Talent Manager's Association (TMA) at talentmanagers.org has a code of ethics and by-laws available online; it defines a talent manager and regulates its members in a self-governing state to ensure quality representation. A listing of members is also posted on their website. Not all managers are members of this organization, and are therefore not required to practice business according to TMA's code of ethics. This site is a valuable resource if you are considering contract agreements with a manager.

6. Legally, agents cannot be producers. Producing their clients' projects is considered a conflict of interest. However, managers are not legally prohibited from producing projects for television and film, and some package their client list. This can get tricky because it can dilute the relationship – who is working for whom? Who is the employer, who is the employee? A producer's job is to keep the cost of production down, including the cost of talent. A rep's job is to negotiate the best money for their client, then score a nice commission from that. A powerful manager/producer can mean it's a big payday for everyone, and a star is comfortable knowing they have someone they trust at the helm. But it can also mean that lesser managers may pressure their clients to engage in crappy projects for crappy pay. And if there is a clause in the contract that prohibits you from terminating the relationship if there is an "offer" of employment, it can get ugly when there's a disagreement over the value of the offer, especially if you don't believe it enhances your career plan.

The main differences between an agent and a manager, however, are more in the contract points regarding commission percentages and the terms of their reach into your services as an actor. To add to the quagmire, there are now also two types of contract offered by agents: the SAG-AFTRA Agency Agreement for franchised agents and "General Service Agreements" (GSAs) for those who aren't franchised. So sifting through all the jargon understandably rattles and strikes fear into the hearts of most actors.

DISCUSSING THE AGENCY AND MANAGER CONTRACT[7]

The first meeting with an agent or manager is usually just a meet-and-greet, and it might be considered bad manners and presumptuous to talk about money. However, if the rep brings it up in the first meeting, or the interest continues to a second meeting with an offer of a contract, then it's fine to discuss money and contract points.

Many actors are uninformed and lack the confidence to ask questions. But it's actually part of the process, so relax, and without defensiveness or fear, ask the agent about commission points and which type of contract they use – a standard SAG-AFTRA Franchised

---

[7] *Disclaimer: The information in this book is current as of the date of publication, to the best of my knowledge. It is not legal advice, I am not an attorney, and I cannot advise you on contracts. I cannot speak on behalf of the Unions and their policies. My purpose is to lend information on basic contract points with simplicity and accuracy, and to the best of my ability. A whole book could be written regarding agency and manager contracts, and it is not within the scope of this section to cover every detail with the depth it deserves – you're getting only the broad strokes. Get final review and professional advice from a licensed entertainment attorney, or the agency relations department of your Union.*

Agency Agreement or a GSA. Know the difference between the two. No matter what they tell you, Agency GSAs and management contracts are not "standard" and special care must be taken to review the fine print.

If they offer you a contract right away, take it home and go over it thoroughly for a few days and get outside assistance to clarify anything you aren't sure about *before* signing. Many contracts can be refined, modified, and negotiated. Look into their background to find out whether there are any legal complaints filed against them. Most often a simple pre-emptive search on IMDb Pro will help you assess whether they have a strong and legitimate clientele, and whether their industry contacts can support your career development.

Many GSAs do not have the same standards and protections for the actor as a SAG-AFTRA franchised agency agreement. An agency GSA should clearly state at the top of the document that it is a State-approved contract. Some, if not most, are modest and very straightforward, almost a replica of the union agreement in terms of commission points and markets, with a moderate expansion of terms. Other GSAs can restrict your legal rights, take higher commissions on everything you earn, and can include sticky termination clauses and even irrevocable check authorizations. It is important that you review the fine print, negotiate for better terms, and decide what is worthy of compromise. If you don't know how to do this, get legal advice from an entertainment attorney, and/or call SAG-AFTRA's agency department (Los Angeles: (323)549-6745; New York (212)827-1444) and provide a copy of the GSA so the union can assist you in reviewing it. Online information is being revised since the merger, so check back regularly at sagaftra.org for updates. Just follow the prompts: Home > Union Info > Agency Relations > News & Advisories, and look for articles like "Your

Relationship with Your Agent." This information is free to all actors. There is also an excellent comparison document in .pdf called "The Fine Print" that compares the standard union agreement with GSAs in both Los Angeles and New York.

THE PATH OF THE MONEY

Generally speaking, the production company usually sends payment within seven to fourteen days after you have wrapped. When check authorizations are executed by you, giving your agent permission to receive monies on your behalf, the agency must deposit those funds into a separate account marked either as "special account" or "client trust account." With respect to all monies earned for TV/Film, the agent has three business days from the time the agency receives the money to cut you a check, minus their commission on the gross.

For television commercials, the agent has five days from the time they receive the money to send you your check, minus their commission on the gross. If you are receiving the monies directly instead of through your agent or manager, you should build a trusting and healthy relationship with them by sending a commission check immediately. It's simple: following the golden rule keeps everybody happy.

CONTRACT POINTS

The SAG-AFTRA Franchised Agency Agreement has long been the established example and precedent of a fair and equitable arrangement between and actor and his agent. It is uniform in its language with every single agency, and has strong protections in place to guard against unethical practices and material breach. Generally speaking, the SAG-AFTRA Franchised Agency Agreement is pro-actor, while GSAs and manager contracts are not "standard" in a uniform language (can vary from agency to agency), and can favor the agent/manager over the actor to varying degrees. Every clause in any contract is important, but there are some key clauses that you should look for and clarify: Length of contract; exclusivity, markets, and territories for representation; definition of your services and in what medium; commission percentages and commissionable work; termination clauses; legal recourse for disputes.

1. LENGTH OF CONTRACT

SAG-AFTRA Franchised Agency Agreement: 12 to 18 months is suggested.

GSA: One to three years.

MANAGERS: One to three years.

2. REACH: Exclusivity, Fields/Mediums, Territories/Markets

SAG-AFTRA: Exclusive representation is standard for Los Angeles, but both exclusive and non-exclusive contracts are available to actors in New York (this means you can have more than one agent on the East Coast.) The union agreement limits the scope of reach by using very specific language naming the territory, and the actor can seek another agent in another city if needed. The contract will also clearly state the field of representation. This will read something like "in the field of film and television broadcast," or "as agent of commercial representation throughout Los Angeles."

GSA: Can also define the reach and scope as above, or not. Some can state exclusivity "throughout the world," "on the worldwide front," or use vague language like "in any capacity in the entertainment industry," which leaves this open to interpretation. This can be negotiated.

MANAGERS: It's a foregone conclusion that you should have only one manager. A few managers will define a limited territory, but most expect you give them exclusivity in all markets, in all capacity, across the board, including the "worldwide" front. This is usually harder to change with a management contract, but it's not impossible. It's also not impossible to live with, if the other clauses are equitable and don't exclude your ability to retain legal counsel.

Something I overheard in a café: "They can't offer you the world. It's not theirs to give." If your agent or manager represents you in "any capacity" on a "worldwide front" and you've signed over exclusive representation, then you've effectively excluded having additional representation in New York or any other regional market. This arrangement might be in your favor if the agency or management firm has the power, connections, and skills to access national and international markets. But if they're really more of a local outfit, this is something you might consider negotiating. Many representatives are completely open to declining commissions on a regional project that a regional agent has worked to get.

3. **DEFINITION OF YOU** as the Actor, and Goods and Services

The State of California defines you, the artist, as *"actors and actresses rendering services on the legitimate stage and in the production of motion pictures, radio artists, musical artists, musical organizations, directors of legitimate stage, motion picture, and radio productions, musical directors, writers, cinematographers, composers, lyricists, arrangers, models, and other artists and persons rendering professional services in the motion picture, theatrical, radio, television and other entertainment enterprises."*

SAG-AFTRA: Very clear in stating that you are an "Actor" or "Actress" or "Performer." It does not include other positions such as lyricist or cinematographer.

GSA: Can swing mild or wild, depending upon the company. Some moderately broaden the definition to include "artist, producer, and any other related capacities in the entertainment industry" and it may be a compromise you can live with. Others throw in everything but the kitchen sink, and claim all goods and services – writer, director, producer, musician, lyricist, author, editor, designer, consultant, cameraman, technician, associate producer, supervisor, executive and in any other capacity in the entertainment, literary, and related fields throughout the world including merchandising, testimonials, advertising, technology ... including your LLC or corporation – not just acting services and the goods that spring from a particular booking or acting role, but every single interest without limitation. If you're basically just an actor, this can be simplified and negotiated.

MANAGERS: Ditto on the above, mild to wild, or vague with "All forms of entertainment and media, including all fields, without limitation." This one is harder to negotiate as most managers expect this, but a compromise can be reached.

4. COMMISSIONS

SAG-AFTRA: 10 percent, with specified limits on the kinds of work and monies earned that are considered commissionable.

If you've signed a SAG-AFTRA franchised agency agreement, there are limits to what kind of work and earnings they can commission, and it cannot result in paying you below minimum union scale. An actor's booking is often negotiated as "Scale + 10 percent" so that the agent's bump still keeps the actor's gross pay at scale. Generally speaking, salary for time worked is commissionable and penalties and reimbursable expenses are not. Examples of standard commissionable points are: Session Fees (the actual work day or week), Audition Overtime, Holding Fees, Looping and Dubbing, Location Pay, Overtime, Travel, and more. Non-commissionable examples are Forced Calls, Per Diem, Turn-Around pay, Wardrobe Allowance, and other similar items. Commissions on residuals are also limited according to the number of the run (rebroadcast), and the ancillary markets. For more details about commissionable standards set by the union, check sag.org/what-commissionable or call their residual department.

GSA: 10 or 15 or 20 percent, depending on the agency. Some observe and employ the Sag Agreement standards regarding what is commissionable work and residuals, others ask for more. If signed to a theatrical agent, this means you pay them only for TV/Film/Stage bookings; if signed to a commercial agent, then their commission is from commercials and advertising projects.

MANAGERS: 15 to 20 percent of any and all monies, all markets, all goods and services, unlimited by minimum "scale," and in all mediums across the board – even if they don't work for you in this area. Yes, this means if a manager got you a booking for a nickel (below scale), you still owe him a piece of that nickel.

Weigh it out. If they are excellent managers and have a strong clientele and clout, if they aggressively submit you on projects and make calls on your behalf, then all commissions might be considered earned. If they work, they should get paid, and the compromise is a good-faith arrangement. If they don't work at all in one area, or if they're a small local company, then you should be able to negotiate. You're not obligated to give it all away, and many managers will still be okay with 5 percent instead of 20 percent on a commercial if they're not working that market anyway. Others agree to lower the commission to 10 percent if your salary exceeds a certain amount, for instance $80,000.

COMMISSIONS TO BOTH AGENTS AND MANAGERS should apply to only those projects booked during the term of your contract. Check the contract for any grandfather clauses that give them commissions for prior work (residuals) done under previous representation, or for any work done with a new agency if you later move on. For any bookings you acquired during the term of the contract, you will continue to owe them commissions. Commission for series work is based on the terms they negotiated. If you later change representation, a new agent may negotiate a "bump" in pay for that same project. The first agent still gets commission on the original terms, and the new agent gets the commission on the "bump."

5. TERMINATION CLAUSES

SAG-AFTRA gives both the actor and the agent the mutual right to break contract, and to do so freely under conditions such as: The actor hasn't earned $3500 in 91 days in commercials; or the actor hasn't *worked* (different from "auditioned") 10 days in a 91-day period, theatrically. All that's required to break contract is a certified letter to the agent and to the union stating you are no longer represented by them. Call your Union office for more information on termination clauses regarding series options and pickups.

Of Note: if you've just signed with an agent or manager, be patient and remember that developing new or unknown talent takes time. Unless it's clear they're unethical or lazy, I can suggest you give them at least 9 months to a year to submit and build up heat before you become dissatisfied and use this 91 day/3 month "out."

GSA: Some GSAs and management contracts do not give the actor the mutual right to break contract if they're unhappy with the arrangement. The language can state that if the actor gets an "offer" of work in 4 months, he then waives his right to terminate. An offer doesn't always translate into actual work and monies earned. Additionally, it voids actors' rights to pass on projects they don't want to do for some reason (e.g. bad writing, weak films, low pay.) Some agents, however, have no problem refining this clause to reflect the SAG-AFTRA terms, or make mutual the right and freedom to terminate.

MANAGERS: Are not standard in their termination clauses. Some managers are simple, work clean, and don't have parameters or conditions on how and why you want to leave – you just send a certified letter.

Others stridently claim exclusive rights into infinity, giving the right to terminate or option a renewal only to themselves, not the actor. It's bizarre how different each management contract can be – definitely not uniform or standard language. So this clause is one that an actor *must* clarify and work to make mutually beneficial for both parties. If the terms are clear and simple for the actor, you will not need legal assistance if either of you decides to part company.

For both GSAs and management contracts, scrutinize the language regarding power of attorney and check authorizations. Make sure you have the ability to terminate those should either of you break contract. If you don't, you may need to seek outside legal counsel to rescind these.

6. LEGAL/JURISDICTIONAL CLAUSES

These passages set forth how legal disputes will be handled and settled, including your ability to arbitrate and mediate.

SAG-AFTRA: Union Agency Relations department can assist you for most matters; also other city and state agencies if it's a serious breach or disagreement.

GSA: The Union Agency Relations department cannot help you with a GSA, only SAG-AFTRA franchised agency agreements. State agencies can help with a State-approved GSA. Be sure you have an arbitration/mediation clause to protect yourself in case of dispute.

MANAGER CONTRACTS: The language can often be confusing, or protects only the manager, so you should protect yourself with arbitration/mediation language in the contract.

Explanation: Agencies are regulated by the State. There are some avenues you can pursue if you have legal problems with an agency: the union, city attorney, consumer protection agencies, the labor board, even the state attorney general in extreme cases. These bodies have answers and resources to assist you and may even act on your behalf, but these are limited with some GSAs. If you do not have an arbitration clause in your agreement and things get ugly, it will mean a civil suit – you bear the expense of hiring legal counsel to represent you. Or, you bear the expense of buying your way out of your contract; either way, the lack of an arbitration or mediation clause can get expensive.

ALL THINGS CONSIDERED

Actors do have rights and protections, but not so much if they sign first and kick up dust about it later. You are legally and personally responsible for any contract you sign, which means it is incumbent upon you and you alone to try and negotiate the best deal possible *before* you sign a GSA or management contract. This includes your check authorizations. Following the guidelines of the SAG-AFTRA franchise agreement is a good starting point. What you sign is what you agree to. Any verbal agreements that change any of the terms are not valid unless also changed in the language of the contract or attached as side letters and amendments.

Cheer up. I've had the good fortune to work with splendid agents and managers, and they are the norm, not the exception. Most contracts are not scary or sweeping in their demands, and most representatives are open to compromise and negotiating the fine print.

So take a deep breath and calm yourself. This is just another part of the learning curve. In the beginning you have to be your own best friend, your own advocate. What's the worst they can say to a request for compromise? "No?" Such a tiny word, only two letters. They have the right to say no, and so do you. Just weigh things out and make informed decisions about any concessions.

UNION ASSISTANCE WITH CONTRACTS

The Actors' unions provide contract assistance to their members. For instance, the agency relations department at SAG-AFTRA frequently assists in reviewing, clarifying, and advising on negotiating GSAs. If you are presented with a GSA, make sure it states at the top that it is a "State Approved Contract." You may contact the union and send a copy for review. You have to be a full union member in good standing; "SAG-Eligible" and non-union talent are not eligible for assistance. SAG-AFTRA does not review modeling or print contracts. Managerial contracts are outside their jurisdiction, so they cannot offer legal advice on those. They will, however, answer general questions that union members have about the manager/performer relationship.

GOOD, BAD, HOW DO YOU KNOW? RED FLAGS

Never sign a contract if they slide a "Take it or leave it, one-time-only offer" across the table on the first meeting. This is a scam – if they don't want you to read it carefully, there's something to hide.

Some reps will send "form letters" asking for a meeting. One form letter I saw had blank lines throughout, such as "Dear _____," with each actor's name and appointment time hastily written into the blank spaces like a mass mailing. This is not a promising sign and indicates lack of professional muscle. You want an agency that contacts you personally.

Reconsider the contract and relationship entirely if the contract has an "in perpetuity" clause attached to commissionable work and power of attorney, or "throughout the universe" regarding reach and exclusivity. This is a very rare occurrence but it has been seen.

Be wary of contractual clauses that require you to reimburse for ordinary office expenses. The cost of doing business includes paperclips, fax machines, and phone calls. Many don't provide receipts or a breakdown of the costs. If they're too broke to buy their own paper, what professional muscle could they possibly offer? There are other circumstances, though, in which reimbursement is reasonable, so work it out.

Some have fantastic websites claiming to be reps but don't actually have a client list. You can check on IMDb Pro for the client list of each agency or management firm.

Location, location, location. You can tell a lot about an agent and manager by the taste, cleanliness, and use of their office space. If it's seedy, understaffed, rundown, or in the boonies, they may lack enough clout to actually help you. If the assistants are surly and bad-tempered, it's a clue – they answer the phones for casting and industry and in their own way are a reflection of you. They may just be having a bad day, maybe not. More information on agency scams is available in the chapter on "Scams."

SCHMACTORS FROM HELL

You think you're frightened by an agent or manager? That works both ways. Read on for tales in the trenches of ding dongs and bloopers from the agency perspective.

"THE ONLY REAL ACTORS ARE FROM NEW YORK"

ONCE UPON A TIME there was a New York stage Actor who was getting fantastic notices when his play traveled to Los Angeles. A very good Agent (we'll call him A+) was keen to represent him after seeing his remarkable performance. Since signing a new client needs unanimous agreement among all the agents, A+ arranged a big meeting so that the Actor could meet the whole company. The Agent was certain his colleagues would be enthusiastic about his discovery. The Actor arrived in board shorts and flip flops, "California" style. Even his shirt was stained and wrinkled. When asked why he was dressed so badly, the New Yorker said he'd heard that California was more laid back and he didn't have time to launder his clothes. Needless to say, the entire Agency was deeply offended by his lack of respect, and his "Point Man" in the Agency, was embarrassed and angry. They kicked him to the curb.

In an Agent's mind, you are also representing the Agency every time you walk into a casting or production office. They have to be able to trust that you will know how to dress appropriately for the interview. If that Actor didn't have the common sense and respect to dress for a basic business meeting, regardless of the coastline, he couldn't be trusted to be appropriate in a casting session either.

The moral of this story is: Dress in upscale casual or business attire for Agency Meetings, and never underestimate the professionalism of the West Coast. Most Industry there are ex-pats from the East Coast.

"MR. PRETTY"

ONCE UPON A TIME there was a gorgeous, funny, and deeply talented new face (Mr. Pretty), fresh out of acting school. Agents were clamoring to represent him and Mr. Pretty eventually signed with a very good boutique. The flaw in this Actor was that he considered himself an "Artiste," an edgy renegade, free from the bondage of the Hollywood machine. He would not check his email and messages for days at a time, and failed to show at several auditions. He also did not leave "book out" dates when he decided to leave town for a couple of weeks, resulting in losing more appointments. Every time he'd failed to show at an audition, the Casting Director got upset and called the Agent, then another Casting Director, and another. The Agency gave a strong and stern first warning, but also gave him the benefit of the doubt. Because he was young and green, and they figured if they spelled it out, he'd mend his ways. "You have to book out when you leave town. You have to check your messages every day. And either pass or confirm your appointments – if you can't make it, then Casting can give your time slot to another deserving actor." Although the dress down offended his mustang spirit, Mr. Pretty agreed to follow their advice and went home. The following week, he left town without booking out. They fired him.

"So What!? Eff you!" railed the Actor. "You can't push me around. I'm gorgeous, funny, and deeply talented." Confident the ex-Agent "had a problem," Mr. Pretty went looking for a new Agent. His past then bit him in the backside. You can guess what was said when agents called casting for a recommendation – the big raspberry and a thumbs down. Actors can't get signed if they've burned that many bridges.

The Moral of this story is: 1. Check your email and telephone daily. 2. Always confirm or pass an appointment. 3. "Book Out" if you leave town. 4. Trust is earned, not given.

"METHOD, NOT MADNESS"

ONCE UPON A TIME I went to visit my agents. I was shocked to find the entire office wrecked and disheveled - broken vases, pictures knocked off the walls, chairs upturned. "Oh My God! Did you get robbed?!" Heavy with anger, my Agent growled, "No. Actors!" Apparently the Agency had interviewed a new Actor (very "real," very "method," very "exciting") and asked him to come back with a two person scene. The Actor returned the following week with a dramatic fight scene – enacted for "real," full out, and literally trashed the entire space. One of the agents had to duck under his desk. (Sigh.) We can guess the rest.

The Moral: Risk and innovation is always exciting, property damage is illegal.

Think these kinds of brash choices through to the end. If you can't control your instrument at a basic meeting, they can't trust you in an audition room, and they certainly won't trust you on a set. Would you take such liberties on hot set? Would you break a desk or a vase that's already been established in masters and previous takes? Destruction is planned to the penny on a set, for multiple takes with breakaway chairs and stunt men. You'll make a mortal enemy of the design team and Show Runner, if you stop production and jack their budget, while they scramble to find the exact replacement. Why face exile and unemployment from a bad reputation?

Accidents happen, sure – but the above was more about the unchecked ego. Hard to believe that I have to tell this story, but it happens more than you think. Hire a fight coordinator if you can't live without your brawl, and only use about a five to ten foot radius within the office. Or, here's a thought - simply choose a different scene. *Technique is there to illuminate, not decimate, the human experience.*

CHAPTER 7

UNIONS

A union affiliation is the mark of a professional, and it's quite difficult to sign with a good agent without it. Working your way toward a union card can be a long but substantially worthwhile goal, and it starts with a professional attitude and work ethic when you're working non-union jobs.

In the beginning, I worked for years under non-union contracts, and on union jobs as a non-union performer. And because the pay was barely sufficient, I exhausted myself holding down two, sometimes three jobs, just to make ends meet. It still took a while even with a union card to quit my day job before I called myself a full-time actor, but union contracts paid substantially more, took me out of poverty, and allowed me a decent standard of living. It also offered medical benefits when I was sick, and protected me from unscrupulous rehearsal hours.

There were several times as a non-union performer that I was hired as a lead or supporting lead, sometimes paid as little as $80 a week (my rent was 6 times that.) And often, when the union performers signed out for the night after a long day of rehearsal, I was required to stay and rehearse, sometimes until 2 o'clock in the morning. Then I'd get up in a few hours, do my day job, then go to rehearsal again. Acting is hard work – don't let anyone tell you otherwise. When you work that hard to "earn your bones," the union card means more than good pay, it means dignity and abiding self-respect. Trust is earned, and I'd earned my place among my peers when I got my union card.

ACTOR UNIONS AND WHAT THEY DO

The main actor unions and an overview of the actors and mediums they represent:

1. SAG-AFTRA: now a combination of the Screen Actors Guild (with jurisdiction over television, film, commercials and more) and the American Federation of Television and Radio Artists (which also handled some scripted television, including sit-coms, PBS, soaps, game shows, news; as well as radio, radio commercials, and voice-overs.) The merger in 2012 was a major event in the evolution to stabilize the future of actors, especially given the changes toward digital media and the web.

2. Actor's Equity Association (AEA) – Stage and Theatre, part of the Four A's.

The basic job of each union is to protect the actor by providing:

1. Minimum salaries
2. Health benefits
3. Fair and safe working conditions
4. Pension and retirement plans

"EARN YOUR BONES"

JOIN THE UNION

I will attempt to lay out the methods to becoming a union member with the current information available at the time of this writing. Because of the recent merger, there may be inevitable modifications, so it's important that you stay assertive and updated directly through the SAG-AFTRA and AEA links provided within this section. In the meantime, here is the information you need to "earn your bones." Note: all information on union websites is free to the actor – you never need to pay for this.

Know this: Non-union actors can audition for and be hired in both union and non-union projects. Union projects are not closed to non-union talent; that's a myth and I'm living proof. Once you are union, however, you *cannot* work on a non-union project.

Here are the basic established methods to join:

1. If you are working as an extra on a union project, and you are offered a speaking or principal role by that producer, then the production company can "bump" you up to a SAG-AFTRA contract. Get copies and keep your paperwork!

2. Buying in to AFTRA is an obsolete practice after the merger. Beware of any paid services still plying that information – they prey on the uninformed newcomer.

3. "Sister" into the union through SAG-AFTRA and AEA. If you are an AEA member for a year, then you can join SAG-AFTRA (and vice versa.) Your membership and dues to the union of origin must be current in order to qualify, and you have to have

worked as a principal under that union's jurisdiction.

4. SAG-AFTRA voucher system (extra work, background player.) Proof of employment as SAG-AFTRA covered background player at full union rates for a minimum of three days. The days need not be consecutive.

5. Equity Membership Candidate program (EMC) – work as a non-union actor or understudy for 50 weeks at an Equity-approved theatre under a LORT/stock/dinner theatre contract. Register as EMC with Equity. These weeks also need not be consecutive.

6. The Taft-Hartley Act is also a way to join the union. This permits a non-union actor to work in a union production up to 30 days without joining. After day 30, you join – or book three jobs as a non-union performer on a union show. I like to call this "Three strikes and you're in."

All of this is do-able. Most of the above is in fact the path that I took to gain my own union cards. With persistence and tenacity, I kept pounding pavement, submitting myself to both union and non-union work. I was lucky enough to work on union shows as non-union talent, first on stage and then on sets. Eventually, I'd built my reputation and skills to garner consistent contracts on stage which led to my AEA card. I was mid-application with AEA to be "sistered in" to SAG, but soon booked my third SAG job and came in under the Taft-Hartley Act. This process took a couple of years and it wasn't easy, but in the meantime I had honed my skills and credits so that I was able to compete with excellence against seasoned professionals.

SAG-AFTRA

Screen Actors Guild and the American Federation of Television And Radio Artists merged in 2012. From the SAG-AFTRA website on how to join:

Eligibility Check: sagaftra.org/join
Steps to Join: sagaftra.org/content/steps-join
Non-Members: sagaftra.org/content/non-member-faq

AEA

If you would like to be a member of Actor's Equity Association (AEA), there's information online at actorsequity.org/membership/howtojoin.asp. AEA is also part of what's called the "Four A's" which has jurisdiction over other contracts for performers such musical artists and variety artists.

SHORTCUTS AND INSIDER TIPS

There are none. However, there are plenty of people willing to sell you "the secret" and "the shortcut." Here are samples of unsavory methods designed to take your money:

Some scammers are offering forged SAG-AFTRA vouchers to help you get a union card. But the union will know the difference, and by then your money is gone and so is your "voucher buddy." Furthermore, if the guild discovers such misconduct on your part (and they will, they always do), you may find yourself subject to disciplinary proceedings, which could result in your being fined, suspended and/or expelled from the guild. It will certainly delay or completely dismantle your ability to join your peers. The shortcut is simply not worth the heat.

There are postings and ads on social networks and/or actor-specific websites by "professional consultants" who will, for only $65 per hour, talk to you about your concerns with joining the union – a bit of professional hand-holding as it were. This was particularly ugly during the merger vote, but I always see it during any time of upheaval in the industry, and these "professionals" prey on fear. I randomly check into the background and credentials of these people on sites like IMDb Pro, the BBB, and other resources, and quite often find no discernible credits that will support a claim as a consultant. Think about it. If their credits are weak or non-existent, what's the value of their advice?

A signature of most scams is the opportunist who buys domain names that are almost like the real McCoy, but operate as a decoy. There was recently a website with a web address almost identical to the new SAG-AFTRA web address, but it was not the union, nor was it endorsed or operated by the union. It was, instead, a website devoted to selling a book; it promised to show you how to get into the union – if you buy the book. Listen. Buy it, don't buy it, up to you, I don't care. Hey, it could be a valuable resource. All I know is that union membership information is free if you simply call or visit the union website directly.

In closing, there really isn't any shortcut to the business of acting, or anything that will replace good old-fashioned, nose-to-the-grindstone work. Even if you did find a magic key to circumvent the system, you'd be an unseasoned amateur competing against well-trained long-timers, actors whose skills will kick you to the curb. So quit whining, roll up your sleeves, and get your hands dirty. Acting is work, hard work. Earn your bones.

CHAPTER 8

SCAMS

HOW DO YOU KNOW IT'S LEGIT?

The industry is saturated with workshops, showcases, specialty classes, con artists, and claims to "catapult your career to the next level." There are also tons of legitimate teachers, coaches, and programs, with similar-sounding ads, offering real services. The difference between the two is that legitimate services are usually ongoing, with traditional settings for their acting classes, and offer learning and instruction, with no promise of employment. That's not to say there aren't good workshops and seminars – there are.

Most legitimate industry representation, workshops, casting calls, production calendars, or audition submission services will be licensed and bonded and can be found on a government database listed later in this section. Good services are often promoted through long-established industry publications such as *The Call*

Sheet, Backstage, Casting Networks, and Breakdown Services/Actors Access, as well as institutions such as the actors' unions. SAG-AFTRA and AEA often host seminars and workshops for their members. If golden opportunities are hawked on neighborhood publications or want ads, be circumspect – the information can be at worst untrue, or at best just weak.

Samuel French and Drama Book Shop also offer resources to help you find legitimate agents, managers, casting, and scams, as well as labels for mailings. SAG-AFTRA and AEA post online listings of agencies that are bonded and franchised.

Another route for fact-checking legitimate agencies and production is IMDb Pro. The Los Angeles Office of the Consumer Protection Division of the Federal Trade Commission, the City Attorney and many other state agencies have a lot of information to protect the actor. You just have to seek it out, and you can start by reading the Krekorian Talent Scam Prevention Act provided at the end of this chapter. Don't be a victim, get informed.

RED FLAGS: The PAY-TO-PLAY and the BAIT-AND-SWITCH

AGENCY/MANAGEMENT FEES

NEVER PAY AN AGENT TO REP YOU – ever. Never pay to take a meeting with one. The legitimate talent agency does not charge a *fee* payable *in advance* for registering you, for resumes, for public relations services, for screen tests, acting lessons or any other services. If you are signed as a client to a legitimate agency, you will pay the agency nothing until you work, and then 10 percent of your earnings as a performer – but nothing in advance.

Commissions – gooooood.
Signing bonus – baaaaaad.[8]

AGENCY/MANAGER "TALENT DEVELOPMENT"

So-called talent development fees are just double-speak; it means you won't have to pay an upfront fee, but you will have to pay to take their mandatory workshops, use only their photographers and labs and coaches, or they won't sign you. This ruse could be a sign of a soft kickback arrangement between these services and the agency. Don't be bamboozled by a threat of getting cut from a client list if you don't use their guy – getting dropped by a crappy agent is a blessing in disguise. A legitimate rep will suggest a list of photographers, or refer you to a list of acting coaches who have good reputations, but they will *never* restrict your right to choose for yourself.

Most of the agency-mandated services and fees can be outrageously expensive and lead nowhere. Why do people fall for it? Because con men don't have horns on their head with a big neon sign flashing "Liar, Cheat, Thief." They look completely harmless, legitimized by glossy websites, and the spin is astonishingly good – they will say all the right things about your look, your talent, and your potential. The spin will also have the right dash of truth to make the lie sound reasonable,

---

[8] *NOTE: The Krekorian Act stipulates that this kind of activity is illegal. Unfortunately, some newcomers to the business have misunderstood the legal terminology within the Act, stated as "Advanced Fee Talent Services," thinking that the actor can pay in advance in order to be represented. Not the case. The Act protects the actor from ever having to pay for representation, before signing, after signing, and at any time, except on commissionable work.*

and they'll promise whatever it takes to get you to sign a check. Sometimes they're caught and forced to close down, but then they simply move down the street and start all over again with a new storefront. So be conscious of the pattern of behavior, not just the name on the shingle.

If you're new and starting out, a decent photographer in L.A. is in the price range of $200 – $465; legitimate workshop fees range from $40 to $75 for a one-nighter, and up to $500 for several nights/weeks and longer hours. Monthly acting classes cost about $250 per month, sometimes more if it's a big school or famous teacher. So tell me, why are you paying several thousand?

ADVERTISEMENTS

Legitimate talent agencies do not advertise for clients in newspaper classifieds nor do they solicit by mail or email. Legitimate personal managers do not advertise for newcomers, nor promise employment.

MANAGEMENT "OFFICE MAINTENANCE"

Some managers actually charge their clients for their miscellaneous small business expenses and overhead. Not a good sign. You do not have to oblige. Reimbursement is suitable only for regular actor expenses that they took care of on your behalf, because you were too busy or unable.

PAY TO "SCREEN TEST"

This is widely practiced, preying on the amateur. The approach runs the gamut of taste – from a slick and polished marketing releases to a basic posting on a telephone pole. Ignore it. If a studio wants an actor for a screen test, they go through an agent, not a street promotion.

PAY TO MEET A "TALENT SCOUT"

With the rapid development of the Internet and demo reel submissions, talent scouts are pretty much a thing of the past. Walk away if you're approached. There are a few rare birds left with legitimate connections – but remember, I got my meeting with a talent scout through my agent, and I certainly didn't pay for the privilege. The audition was just like a regular casting call – I went in with two prepared monologues, they taped it, and I went home.

PAY-TO-PLAY REALITY SHOWS

"This is your big break if you have fifty dollars." Some recruiters will approach you directly to pitch that you can become the next big reality star. Or, they market with a glossy talent search program, claiming the opportunity to be seen by hundreds, even thousands of directors, producers, and casting directors. When the actors follow up, they've disappeared – no phone line, email, or office at the physical address. In the meantime, hundreds of actors have already sent in applications with their fees. This is a classic bait-and-switch.

BACKGROUND "EXTRAS" CASTING COMPANIES

These outfits ask for a $25+ fee to hold your place in a national database. For the money, you are listed and then contacted if and when a movie shoots in your area. Some even go further and claim a project is now casting, then solicit your headshot and resume for another fee to attend the audition. Once they collect the money, the bank account is closed and the audition is cancelled. These scams are normally conducted in out-of-state regions where it's difficult to send a union rep to follow up. SAG-AFTRA protects extras, too, and has a listing of legitimate projects in production. Contact SAG-AFTRA with any questions regarding out-of-state productions if you are approached to participate in one. One legitimate casting source for background work is Central Casting.

STAR IN AND PRODUCE YOUR OWN MOVIE

Every once in a while, there is an ad placed offering you a part in a movie and the added bonus to be a producing partner if you contribute toward financing the film. Report these ads immediately to SAG-AFTRA.

MODELING AGENCIES SEEKING NEW FACES

These ads usually claim "NO EXPERIENCE NECESSARY" and are not usually found in established industry publications, but outside in local news rags or sites like Craigslist. (Some legitimate projects are posted to Craigslist, but this site is largely unscreened or vetted.) Many times it's really just a front to sell very expensive workshops, photo sessions, and other services. Some actors are asked to attend a meeting in a vacant office building, or asked to send topless photos for casting body doubles for famous actors in films requiring love scenes.

The victims of the above practices are not restricted to just women – men are potential prey as well. The consequences range from minor, to mortified, to fatal. Here's my suggestion: if you think the modeling offer or appointment is real, but are still uncertain, practice the buddy system and take a friend. If anything seems off, leave immediately. Generally, a legitimate meeting will take place at a real production/agency address, and during business hours – not at night, in a remote district or a private residence. There's a cautionary tale on the death of Kristi Johnson, *Death in the Hollywood Hills*, by correspondent Keith Morrison at: nbcnews.to/ONgtP3.

WORKSHOPS, SHOWCASES AND ONLINE WEBINARS

Casting workshops are legal. They just have to comply with the new laws in order to stay legal. There is quite a bit of controversy and debate about the value of casting workshops and agency showcases. Some consider it unethical to pay to be seen by industry people, and others have no problem paying for the opportunity – if it is indeed a real opportunity. Before 2010, there was an epidemic of workshops advertising a famous casting person, agency, or movie studio executive, some charging enormous fees. But on the magic night, someone else from the casting or agency office showed up in their place instead – like the phone receptionist, an assistant, and even pretenders with no ties whatsoever to the company they touted.

Actors have the choice to attend these events, and to spend their money to do so – but they pay to meet the real McCoy, not a stand-in, so this practice is considered a bait-and-switch. Additionally, the marketing ads directly or indirectly offer the hope or promise of future employment, which is in direct violation of the labor laws. Since 2010, the Los Angeles City Attorney has worked hard to crack down on scam workshops whose only purpose is to take your money.

Before you take a workshop, do a little homework. First, read the additional document after this chapter, the "Krekorian Talent Scam Prevention Act," outlining the limits of what legitimate workshops and showcases can offer, regulations, and what services are prohibited by law. Then go to 1.usa.gov/NLru5V for the DLSE listing. Legitimate workshop and showcase venues will be listed as bonded under "Fee Related Talent Service Bonds." You can also search for talent agencies licenses on the same menu under "Talent Agency License Database." You can also go to Samuel French or Drama Book Shop and buy a "Scam" publication warning of the current ruses. Lastly, search the internet to see if there's any truth to their industry connections, and study ads to compare the regular rates of other classes and workshops. Scammers often jack the cost, charging thousands of dollars – money that could be spent on better things.

A good solid casting workshop will be licensed and bonded, and divulge in advance whether the actual casting director or the casting associate will be in attendance. The fees charged are now on a sliding scale according to the status of the industry professional – anywhere from $30 to $75. In some acting circles, meeting a casting associate for $30 can sound like a good idea, especially if their office casts big shows and your mailings aren't getting their attention. I don't disagree, I just want actors to get what they pay for. I also believe a good agent will get you an introduction to a casting office just as well.

By law, they cannot promise you employment. If the workshop is designed and executed to teach you the ropes of auditioning, camera technique, script breakdown, etc., then technically it's not an audition, and you may/may not learn some good things. I, personally, do not attend these – I think it's my agent's job to get me in the room. If you choose to sign up, my best advice is to go in with the attitude that you are there primarily to experience growth, just like you would for any class. Yes, they see new talent, and yes you get to shake a few hands and network, but never assume you will be discovered or book a job from it – you'll sleep better at night and the money you spend will be a conscious decision, not an act of desperation.

BREAKDOWNS AND CASTING SUBMISSION SCAMS

In Chapter 4, Breakdown Services, Casting Networks, Now Casting, Casting Frontier and Backstage were discussed; these companies are long-established and credible in their services to the entertainment industry. That's not to say there aren't others. However, in an era of start-up companies eager to get a piece of the action, it's difficult to know the difference between the young, legitimate competitors and the scammers. Be careful of any copycats that mimic the casting sites above; check their track record and credentials before signing up.

The scammers host submission sites built only to take your money, not build your career. Through skillful web building, the scammers really do look like the real thing online; they offer competitive price breaks, and even their breakdowns appear legitimate. If the site is a scam, a couple of things generally happen:

- You send your materials to a real project, but your submission doesn't actually make it to the casting office – it evaporates in to ethernet limbo as it's delivered to a dummy address. Or,

215

- The casting opportunity is a "late break" – it's real, but a week or two old. So the window of opportunity has actually passed you by.

Additionally, some people offer the daily, original breakdowns that agents and managers receive, running an underground network to actors who don't have access to the big shows. This is illegal and Breakdown Services routinely places dummy projects designed to catch actors using underground breakdowns. Occasionally, people are caught, and they pay very big fines. It's a risky enterprise.

IN CLOSING

There are bad guys everywhere in the world, spoiling the fun for the rest of us good citizens. I would like to add that, in my experience, most of the people I have met or worked with in New York and Los Angeles are solid, creative professionals, whose only desire is to work and be good at it. The above information is to help you avoid losing time and money so you can move smoothly forward and find the right people, people who can actually help you. Stay sharp, do your homework, and make informed decisions. Aggressively pursue the acting, modeling and talent scam alert websites, such as SAG-AFTRA/Scams, BizParentz, ActorsInfoBooth, the FTC (Federal Trade Commission), Info4Actors (also visit their BEST and WORST tabs), and others.

Remember: there are no victims, only volunteers.

KREKORIAN TALENT SCAM PREVENTION ACT

I have discussed several ways in which grifts, at best unethical, at worst illegal, have been operating in the Los Angeles market and elsewhere. In 2009, the State of California passed legislation called The Krekorian Talent Scam Prevention Act which was designed to bolster current labor law and introduce new language to broaden its scope and enforceability. Its main targets were fake casting workshops, fake agency showcases, and pay-to-play agents and managers who charged fees for representation. Using this legislation, the Los Angeles City Attorney's Office quickly cleaned up scams that emptied the wallets of unsuspecting actors.

The Krekorian Act doesn't mean that this blight has been entirely eliminated, but it has made massive shifts in the market and required showcases, workshops, and agents to advertise properly and operate more cleanly. What follows is the letter of July 2010, from the Los Angeles City Attorney's office. Please read it and stay current with your rights and the law.

City Hall East
200 N. Main Street
Room 500
Los Angeles, CA 90012

(213) 978-8070 Tel
(213) 978-8111 Fax
atty.talent@lacity.org

CARMEN A. TRUTANICH
City Attorney

July 1, 2010

The purpose of this letter is to inform you that groundbreaking new laws regulating the talent service industry became effective January 1, 2010. <u>These laws affect a broad range of businesses, including acting schools, casting workshops, website listing services, representation services, website listing services and call-in services, to name just a few</u>.

This notice is being sent to a large number of talent services to ensure industry-wide understanding of the new laws and to obtain maximum compliance. Your selection as a recipient of this letter is not necessarily indicative of any wrongful past conduct.

The new laws, known as "*The Krekorian Talent Scam Prevention Act of 2009*," are found in Chapter 4.5 of the Labor Code, entitled "Fee-Related Talent Services." They are available in their entirety at www.leginfo.ca.gov. First, click on "California Law." Then, click on "Labor Code." Then scroll down (on the right side) to Sections 1701 through 1705.

<u>Please note that "lack of knowledge" is not a defense to a criminal violation of these laws</u>. A willful violation of any provision by a talent service, its owner, officer, agent, director, agent or employee is punishable as a misdemeanor, with a maximum penalty for each offense <u>of one year in county jail and a fine of $10,000.</u> (See Labor Code §1704.) Failure to comply fully can also result in a civil enforcement action. Further, a victim injured by a violation of this Chapter may bring an action to recover damages and or restrain and enjoin a violation, and is statutorily entitled to no less than three times the amount paid to the service and to attorney's fees and costs.

218

The following is a brief overview of the new laws and is not intended to relieve you of your obligation to read and understand Labor Code Chapter 4.5 in its entirety. Any inaccuracy or omission in this overview may not be relied upon by you as a defense to any violation of this Chapter.

Chapter 4.5 of the Labor Code divides the fee-related talent service industry into four (4) categories:

1. **Advance Fee Talent Representation Services** → Now Prohibited
2. **Talent Training Services** → Permitted, must comply with regulations
3. **Talent Counseling Services** → Permitted, must comply with regulations
4. **Talent Listing Services** → Permitted, must comply with regulations

ADVANCE FEE TALENT REPRESENTATION SERVICE ("AFTRS"): Labor Code §1702: No "person" shall own, operate, act in the capacity of, advertise, solicit for, or knowingly refer a person to an AFTRS. (For the list of exemptions, see Labor Code §1702.4.)

"Person" means an individual, company, society, firm, partnership, association, corporation, limited liability company, trust, or other organization (Labor Code 1701(e)).

Per Labor Code §1701.1 an AFTRS is defined as follows:
1. Provides an artist (or)
   offers to provide an artist (or)
   advertises as providing an artist (or)
   represents itself as providing an artist

2. Directly (or)
   by referral to another person

3. With any one of the following services:

   • procuring or attempting to procure an employment opportunity or an engagement as an artist (or)

   • procuring or attempting to procure an audition (or)

- procuring or attempting to procure a talent agent or talent manager, including an associate, representative or designee of a talent agent or talent manager (or)

- managing or directing the development of an artist's career

[NOTE: "Audition" is defined in Labor Code §1701(b):

"**Audition**" means any activity for the purpose of obtaining employment, compensated or not, as an artist whereby an artist meets with, interviews or performs before, or displays his or her talent before, any person, including a producer, a director, or a casting director, or an associate, representative, or designee of a producer, director, or casting director, who has, or is represented to have, input into the decision to select an artist for an employment opportunity. An "audition" may be in-person or through electronic means, live or recorded, and may include a performance or other display of the artist's promotional materials."

[NOTE: "Employment opportunity" is defined in Labor Code §1701(c):

"**Employment opportunity**" means the opportunity to obtain work as an artist, <u>whether compensated or not</u>.]

4. <u>And</u> charges or receives a <u>fee</u> ** from, or on behalf of an artist for:

- any of the services listed in paragraph (3), above (or)

- photographs, Internet Web sites, or other reproductions or other promotional materials as an artist (or)

- lessons, coaching, seminars, workshops, or similar training for an artist (or)

- any other product or service required for the artist to obtain from or through the AFTRS any of the services listed in paragraph (3), above.

[**NOTE**: ** "**Fee**" is defined in Labor Code §1701(d). If a talent service does not charge or receive a fee, then it is not an AFTRS. Labor Code §1701(d)(1) through (4) lists the categories that are not considered "fees," including, among others, "a percentage of income earned by the artist for his or her employment as an artist (e.g., "commissions") and verifiable "reimbursements for out-of-pocket costs" paid to independent third parties.]

TALENT COUNSELING SERVICE (TCS):
A person may operate a TCS, but must comply with Labor Code §1703. (For the list of exemptions, see Labor Code §1703.6)

Per Labor Code §1701(f), a TCS is defined as follows:

1. For a fee from, or on behalf of, the artist

2. Provides an artist (or)
   offers to provide an artist (or)
   advertises as providing an artist (or)
   represents itself as providing an artist

3. Directly (or)
   by referral to another person

4. With career counseling, vocational guidance, aptitude testing, or career evaluation as an artist, coaching, seminars, workshops, or similar training

5. And does not manage or direct the development of that artist's career. [**NOTE**: If the person does this, then that person is an AFTRS, which is prohibited by Labor Code §1702]

TALENT LISTING SERVICE (TLS):
A person may operate a TLS, but must comply with Labor Code §1703 (For the list of exemptions, see Labor Code §1703.6)

Per Labor Code §1701(g) a TLS is defined as follows:

1. For a fee from, or on behalf of, the artist

2. Provides an artist (or)
   offers to provide an artist (or)
   advertises as providing an artist (or)
   represents itself as providing an artist

3. Directly (or)
   by referral to another person

4. With any of the following:

   - A list of one or more auditions or employment opportunities (or)

   - A list of talent agents or talent managers, including an associate, representative, or designee thereof (or)

   - A search of any database for an audition or employment opportunity, or a database of talent agents or talent managers, or an associate, representative, or designee thereof (or)

   - Providing the artist with the ability to perform a self-directed search of any database for an audition or employment opportunity, or a database of talent agents or talent managers, or an associate, representative, or designee thereof (or)

   - Storage or maintenance for distribution or disclosure to a person represented as offering an audition or employment opportunity, or to a talent agent or to a talent manager or an associate, representative, or designee of a talent agent or talent manager of either of the following:

     A. An artist's name, photograph, Internet Web site, filmstrip videotape, audition tape, demonstration reel, resume, portfolio, or other reproduction or promotional material of the artist (or)

B. An artist's schedule of availability for an audition or employment opportunity

[NOTE: This includes a "call-in" service]

TALENT TRAINING SERVICE (TTS):
A person may operate a TTS, but must comply with Labor Code §1703 (For the list of exemptions, see Labor Code §1703.6)

A TTS is permitted to operate, but must comply with Labor Code §1703

Per Labor Code §1701(j) a TTS is defined as follows:

1. For a fee from, or on behalf of, the artist

2. Provides an artist (or)
   offers to provide an artist (or)
   advertises as providing an artist (or)
   represents itself as providing an artist

3. Directly (or)
   By referral to another person

4. With lessons, coaching, seminars, workshops, or similar training

[NOTE: A "workshop" is specifically included in the definition of a TTS. However, a workshop that offers auditions or employment qualifies as an "Advance Fee Talent Representation Service," which is prohibited by Labor Code §1702.]

RULES APPLYING TO TALENT SERVICES (TCS, TLS, TTS):

CONTRACTS:
A TCS, TLS and TTS must comply with the following requirements pertaining to contracts. A TCS, TLS and TTS contract shall:

1. Be provided to the artist to keep before the artist sings the contract and before becoming obligated to pay any fee (<u>Exception</u>: A contract executed through the Internet, provided it is available to be downloaded and copied)
   Labor Code §1703(i)

2. Be single document, in writing, and in at least 10-point type
   Labor Code §1703(a), Labor Code §1703(d)

3. Include the name, address, phone, fax (if any), website (if any), email (if any) of <u>all</u> of the following:
   The talent service (and)
   The talent service's representative executing the contract (and)
   The artist
   Labor Code §1703(a)(1)

4. Describe the services to be performed and when they are to be performed
   Labor Code §1703(a)(2)

5. Describe the duration of the contract (which may not exceed 1 year and may not be automatically renewed)
   Labor Code §1703(a)(2), §1703(f)

6. State the amount of fees charged or collected from, or on behalf of an artist and the date(s) those fees are due
   Labor Code §1703(a)(4)

7. Provide evidence of compliance with the applicable bonding requirement, including the name of the bonding company, the bond number (if any), and a statement that a $50,000 bond must be filed with the Labor Commissioner
   Labor Code §1703(a)(3)

8. Include the "Notice Statement" <u>exactly</u> as it appears in Labor Code §1703(a)(5) <u>in bold type and in close proximity to the artist's signature</u>

[NOTE: This language serves notice as to what type of talent service you are operating, informs the artist that only a licensed talent agent can procure work, that your service cannot offer to obtain auditions or employment, advises the artist where to make a complaint and describes the cancellation and refund procedures.]
Labor Code §1703(a)(5)

9. Disclose whether a refund may be obtained after the 10-day cancellation period has expired

[NOTE: Failure to include this statement allows an artist to cancel the contract at any time after the 10-day cancellation period and receive a pro rata refund.]
Labor Code §1703(a)(6)

10. (For talent services that offer to list or display information about an artist, including a photograph, on the service's Internet Web site, or on a Web site which the talent service has authority to design or alter):
    A. Notify the artist that the talent service will remove all Internet listings, photographs and content about an artist within 10 days of a request (and)

    B. Provide the valid telephone number, mailing address and email address where the artist may make such a request
Labor Code §1703(c)

11. Be signed and dated by the artist and the talent service representative executing the contract on behalf of the artist (Exception: A contract executed through the Internet, provided the talent service enables the artist to acknowledge receipt of the contract terms before acknowledging agreement thereto)
Labor Code §1703(b)

[NOTE: Non-complying contracts are voidable by the artist at any time without any penalty whatsoever, per Labor Code §1703(d)]

CANCELLATIONS AND REFUNDS:
A TCS, TLS and TTS must comply with the following requirements pertaining to cancellation and refund procedures:

1. Advise any person inquiring about cancellation to follow the written procedures for cancellation set forth in the contract
   Labor Code §1703(h)

2. Permit cancellation and full refund within 10 business days from the date the artist commences utilizing the services
   Labor Code §1703(e)(1)

3. Provide a pro rata refund after the expiration of the 10-day cancellation period (unless the contract conspicuously discloses that cancellation if prohibited after the 10-day period)
   Labor Code §1703(e)(2)

4. Accept cancelation by mail, delivery, fax (or by the Internet if the contract was executed in whole or in part through the Internet)
   Labor Code §1703(e)(1)

5. Maintain an address for cancellation and notify the artist in writing of any change (may notify artist by email if the artist so designates the email address in the contract)
   Labor Code §1703(g)

6. All refunds must be made within ten (10) business days after delivery of the cancellation notice
   Labor Code §1703(e)(1)

BONDING REQUIREMENTS:
A TCS, TLS and TTS must comply with the following:

1. File a $50,000 bond with the Labor Commissioner (or a deposit in lieu thereof per Code of Civil Procedure §995.710)
    Labor Code §1703.3(a)

    [NOTE: This requirement is <u>not</u> satisfied by the filing of a talent agent bond or by the filing of an employment agency, employment counseling or job listing service bond (See Labor Code §1703.3(a)(10)]

2. File the required bond or deposit <u>prior</u> to advertising or engaging in business
    Labor Code §1703.3(a)

    [NOTE: For more information about where to file the bond, contact Jeanie McBride, Office of the State Labor Commissioner at (415) 703-4846.]

REQUIREMENT TO MAINTAIN AND PROVIDE
DESIGNATED RECORDS TO LAW ENFORCEMENT:
A TCS, TLS and TTS must comply with the following:

Keep the following records for inspection and a true copy furnished, Monday through Friday between the hours of 9 a.m. through 5 p.m. inclusive, except legal holidays, to a peace officer, the Labor Commissioner, the Attorney General, or any district attorney or city attorney
Labor Code §1703.1(b)
The designated records to be kept:

1. Re: Talent Service ownership:
    The name, address, date of birth, social security number, federal tax identification number, and driver's license number and state of issuance thereof, of the owner of the talent service and of its corporate officers (if it is owned by a corporation)
    Labor Code §1703.1(a)(9)

2. <u>Re: Talent Scouts:</u> ("talent scout" is defined in Labor Code §1701(h))
   For every talent scout:
   A. The legal name, principal residence address, date of birth, driver's license number and state of issuance (and)
   B. The name each talent scout uses while soliciting artists
   [NOTE: No two talent scouts for a service may use the same name, per Labor Code §1703.5]
   Labor Code §1703.1(a)(10)

3. <u>Re: Artists</u>
   For each artist contracting with the talent service:
   A. The name and address of each artist under contract (and)
   B. The amount of fees paid by each artist during the term of the contract (and)
   C. The <u>original</u> executed contract for each artist
   [NOTE: Labor Code §1703(j) requires this document be maintained at the service's principal place of business.]
   Labor Code §1703.1(a)(1), §1703.1(a)(2), §1703.1(a)(5)

4. Re: Advertisements:
   • Regarding any advertisement or representation that expressly or impliedly offers an artist the opportunity to meet with or audition before any producer, director, casting director, or any associate thereof, or any other person who makes, or is represented to make, decisions for the process of hiring artists for employment as an artist, or any talent agent or talent manager, or any associate, representative, or designee thereof, <u>written evidence of the supporting facts, including but not limited to</u>:
     A. The name business address, and job title of all persons conducting the meeting or audition (and)

B. The title of the production and the name of the production company
Labor Code §1703.1(a)(6)

• Regarding any advertisement or representation that any artist, whether identified or not, has obtained an audition, employment opportunity, or employment as an artist in whole or in part by use of the talent service, <u>written evidence of the supporting facts, including but not limited to</u>:
   A. The name of the artist (and)
   B. The approximate dates the talent service was used by the artist
Labor Code §1703.1(a)(7)
[<u>NOTE</u>: For definitions of "audition" and "employment opportunity" see Labor Code §1701(b) and §1701(c)]

5. <u>Re: Listings (*Required to be kept by a Talent Listing Service only*)</u>:
   A. A copy of all original listings (and)
   B. The name, business address, and business telephone number of the person granting permission to the talent listing service to use the listing (and)
   C. The date the permission was granted
Labor Code §1703.1(a)(8)

6. <u>Re: Proof Relating to Claimed Exemptions From This Chapter 3.5</u>
   A. Proof that fees paid by an artist to the talent service were actually advanced or owed to a third party having no direct or indirect financial interest in the talent service and that the talent service received no referral fee from that third party (See Labor Code §1701(d)(2))
Labor Code §1703.1(a)(3)

   B. Proof that 90% of the service's student body is post-compulsory high school age, including the student's name, date of birth, principal residence address, principal

telephone number, driver's license number and dates of attendance (See Labor Code §1703.6)
Labor Code §1703.1(a)(4)

7. <u>Any other information required by the Labor Commissioner.</u>
Labor Code §1703.1(a)(11)

<u>ADVERTISING AND SOLICITATIONS:</u>
A TCS, TLS and TTS must comply with the following:

1. <u>Disclaimer required</u>: A written or verbal solicitation or advertisement for an artist to perform or demonstrate any talent for the talent service, or to appear for an interview with the talent service, shall include the following clear and conspicuous statement:
"This is not an audition for employment or for obtaining a talent agent or talent management."
Labor Code §1703.1(b)

2. Must maintain and disclose written evidence supporting certain advertisements and representations (See section above)
Labor Code §1703.4(a)(1)
Labor Code §1703.4(a)(2)

3. General prohibition against false or misleading advertising
Business and Professions Code §17500
(referenced in Labor Code §1705.1)

4. *<u>(Applicable to a Talent Listing Service only):</u>*
A TLS may not make include the trademark, logo, name, word or phrase of a company or organization (including a studio, production company, network, broadcaster, licensed talent agency, labor union, or organization defined in Labor Code §1117) that falsely or misleadingly suggests that company or

organization endorses, sponsors, approves or is
affiliated with that TLS
Labor Code §1703.4(c)(3)

ADDITIONAL PROHIBITED ACTS:
A TCS, TLS and TTS, its owners, directors, officers, agents
and employees may not do any of the following:

1. Charge or attempt to charge an artist for an audition
   or employment opportunity
   Labor Code §1703.4(a)(3)

2. Charge or attempt to charge an artist any fee not
   disclosed in the contract
   Labor Code §1703.4(a)(5)

3. Require an artist, as a condition for using the talent
   service or to obtain an additional benefit or
   preferential treatment from the talent service, to pay a
   fee for:
   - A. Photographs, filmstrips, videotapes,
     audition tapes, demonstration reels, or
     other reproductions of the artist, Internet
     Web sites, casting or talent brochures, or
     other promotional materials in order for the
     artist to use the talent service (or)
   - B. Any product or service in which the talent
     service, its owners, directors, officers,
     agents, or employees has a direct or
     indirect financial interest
   Labor Code §1703.4(a)(4)
   Labor Code §1703.4(a)(7)

4. Refer an artist to any person charging the artist a fee
   for a product or service in which the talent service,
   its owners, directors, officers, agents, or employees
   have a direct or indirect financial interest, <u>unless</u> it is
   conspicuously disclosed in a separate writing for the
   artist to keep, prior to the execution of the contract.
   Labor Code §1703.4(a)(6)

5. Accept compensation or consideration for referring an artist to any person charging that artist a fee.
Labor Code §1703.4(a)(8)

6. Within 10 days of delivery of a request, failing to remove an artist's information or photograph from the talent service's Internet Web site or a Web site it has authority to design or alter.
Labor Code §1703.4(a)(9)

7. Attempt to have an artist waive his or her rights under this Chapter (Chapter 3.5)
Labor Code §1705.2

8. _(Only Applicable to a Talent Counseling Service (TCS) and a Talent Training Service (TTS)_:
A TCS and a TTS, its owners, officers, directors, agents, and employees may not own, operate or have a direct or indirect financial interest in a talent listing service
Labor Code §1703.4(b)

9. _(Only Applicable to a Talent Listing Service (TLS)_:
A TLS, its owners, officers, directors, agents, and employees:
    A. May not own, operate or have a direct or indirect financial interest in a talent counseling service or a talent training service (and)
    B. May not provide a listing of an audition, job or employment opportunity without written permission for the listing (and without keeping and maintaining specified records)
Labor Code §1703.4(c)(1)
Labor Code §1703.4(c)(2)

10. No talent scout shall use the same name as used by any other talent scout soliciting for the same talent service.
Labor Code §1703.5

11. No talent service shall permit a talent scout to use the same name as used by any other talent scout soliciting for the talent service.
Labor Code §1703.5

END OF SUMMARY

To reiterate, all appropriate efforts should be made to ensure full compliance with the requirements of state law described above. The City Attorney's Office is monitoring the talent service industry closely, and reserves the right to take any criminal or civil enforcement action necessary to abate and punish violations of these laws.

Please understand that public prosecutors are not authorized to provide private legal counsel, such as reviewing or approving the operation of a particular talent service.

Very truly yours,
CARMEN A.
TRUTANICH
Los Angeles City
Attorney

By

MARK LAMBERT
Deputy City
Attorney
Consumer
Protection Section

CHAPTER 9

LEGAL RESOURCES

Check the State Bar Association or Better Business Bureau when hiring an attorney to see whether there are complaints against them. To the best of my knowledge, the following are highly regarded:

CALIFORNIA LAWYERS FOR THE ARTS (C.L.A.): Offers referral services for legal consultation to creative artists, organizations, and arts-related legal matters for a fraction of the cost. calawyersforthearts.org

PARASEC (PARACORP): For actors and artists interested in business or incorporating: parasec.com

SAG-AFTRA Agency Relations and Legal Department reviews agency contracts

ENTERTAINMENT ATTORNEY (INDEPENDENT COUNSEL):
A. Chandler Warren - (323) 876-6400
email: AChandlerWarren@aol.com

AVVO: Rating/Rreferral site for entertainment attorneys
avvo.com/entertainment-lawyer/ca/los_angeles.html

IMMIGRATION ATTORNEY: The following referrals were
made by colleagues of mine from Europe and Canada.

1) Ralph Ehrenpreis

   1880 Century Park East
   Suite 550
   Los Angeles CA 90067
   (310)553-6600
   ralphehrenpreis.com
   email: info@ralphehrenpreis.com

2) Pamela Forrester

   468 N. Camden Dr.
   Suite 268N
   Beverly Hills CA 90210
   (310)785-9531
   valentelaw.net
   email: pamelaf@valentelaw.net

3) Barnhard P. Wolfsdorf

   1416 2nd Street
   Santa Monica CA 90401
   (310)570-4088
   wolfsdorf.com
   email: visalaw@wolfsdorf.com

CHAPTER 10

NOTES FROM
THE OPEN ROAD

NO GOOD PLAY IS ABOUT YOU

Actors today need to know how to do it all – stage, film, television – and therefore be mindful of the rhythm, tempo, and style (like a fingerprint) that each writer and genre possesses. Many actors think that writers write words, and playing them "realistically" is all one needs. The truth is that writers write *ideas*, and there are different forms of realism, so actors mustn't play them as if they are all the same. There is an obvious difference between Williams and Pinter; between *The Office* and *Boardwalk Empire;* film noir and madcap farce. Going for the truth is always wanted, but the style of the play will give it its shape. Know your form, know your audience.

"In real life, people talk about what they know,
not what someone wrote for them." ~ Stella Adler

"Knowingness" ... is not about the mind, it's about experience – forming a physical, psychological, and emotional experience that brings the character so close to me that I can display the character from the inside out. If successful in that work, it'll engage me in an effortless freefall of "living." I can't say I've always been successful in the requirements of my craft, but I have never forgotten my obligation to it. The single most empowering skill I learned from Stella Adler was that of script analysis. It's a very straightforward approach to a script, requiring time and discipline, and in time it became second nature to me – allowing me to work hard, fast, and deep on any script at any time. It gives me questions to ask, lets the script answer them, and allows me to create a sense of ownership of my work. The best part is that I rarely have problems learning my lines. Rote memorization is for amateurs. You can disagree and go rote, but remember that 500 other actors are also memorizing their lines. If you want more than rote, you don't have to have the answers, just the right questions. The answers are already in the script if you know what to look for.

"No good play is about you." ~ Stella Adler

The process begins by *letting the script work me*, not the other way around. The words and the mind are there, but only as a trigger to activate my gut, my instincts. I must use my mind to find the themes of the story and the past of the characters so that the audience can see me (as the character) in continuation of my life. I then envision and play out the clues from the script, creating active experiences I can use to reveal the character as an individual. No one can tell you when the thought ends and the feelings begin – the experience is seamless and happens in just a fraction of a second – and so does your acting moment.

A writer is deliberate in his choices, his themes, his relationships – it's my job to find them, lift them, and embrace them. Consciously approach a part looking for the themes and the implied past that the writer has given. You cannot play Chekhov without a past – if you go to the words, you will fail. For a more contemporary example, look at the dialogue in the opening scene of "Babel" between Susan and Richard (beautifully played by Cate Blanchett and Brad Pitt) – the number of words on the page are practically poverty stricken. This scene is complex and impossible to play without the past, without the tension of the play's larger themes of language and its inadequacy, and the larger language that resonates in the common human experience: loneliness, humiliation, betrayal, abandonment, failure, death, innocence, madness, temptation, mercy, and parenthood. The experience of any one of these is beyond the scope of language, whether it's the isolation shown through the desert terrain of a Moroccan home or the arid longings of a man's soul. These are just a few of the beautiful and terrifying ideas of "Babel." So we must learn to speak intimately, without words, and reach for the enormous yet common, humanity that unites us all.

Script Analysis asks even more questions about the circumstances of who, where, and what you are – and the script will always give you the clues. All this work then leads you to a point of departure to fall willingly into the unknown (what I call "the ride") and navigate emotional and psychological waters. The sooner you hone the skills of digging out the script, the better. Because, one day, you will encounter a role in which lists of actions will not help you, in which objectives and obstacles will not come to your aid, and where character traits defy reason. Something larger must take over, and you will leave your lists behind. But you'll be ready – because the demands of the search will have built the actor muscle necessary to survive the ride. Then you'll discover that the greatest thing about free-falling without a net is that you won't need one. That's ... a really ... cool ... ride.

Carpe Diem, Little Warriors! and Break 'Em, Baby!

TAKING A MEETING VS. A CALLBACK

A meeting is different from a callback. A callback still requires the actor to do their pages again. In the callback, be effortless and comfortable with your character. Don't change your acting choices, because that's what got you the callback. But do hone them for depth and fluidity. A meeting, however, is a pow-wow between a director or producer and the actor in the running for a lead or supporting lead. However, the actor does not read for the part.

Traditionally, a meeting is usually with a high-profile name and the production team is looking to get a green light for financing as well as generate excitement through the star's talent. But if you're brand new to this process and working your way up the ranks of Indie films, here are a some pointers about the meeting itself.

The meeting is a conversation with a couple of functions: a getting-to-know-you part, and then discussions about the project itself. Both of you figure out whether you're compatible with one another and how you each plan to approach and interpret the script when shooting. ALWAYS REMEMBER: PEOPLE HIRE PEOPLE, NOT PROMOTERS. Stay real, no hard sells.

GETTING TO KNOW YOU:

Practice beforehand as if they've asked you questions about yourself – both personal and professional. Stay away from negative facts. They don't care about divorces, breakups, car accidents, injuries, bad mothers and crooked Agents. If it comes up, be ready with a positive spin, a benign and supportive deflection. Then change the subject back to the project.

In talking about yourself personally, have some short stories/quips, hobbies, interesting things ready. Stay away from politics, sex, and religion. In telling them about yourself in professional ways, let them lead the question, and don't start "selling" yourself. Be ready with two or three short quips about some project on your resume. They may never ask, but you'll feel ready.

The art of conversation is to get people to speak about themselves. Do your research. Look up your director or producers on IMDb, find their titles, watch their projects, and read their bios. It will definitely give you lots to talk about. Now the other part they assess is your skill and focus as a Lead with the script (which of course you've read before the meeting, right?)

Your script preparation is key. After reading the script, note specific research you might want to talk about to develop the role. Examples include: dialects, time/era/epic, themes, conflict, profession, disabilities, comedic style, and genre. Your director probably also has a "look" he's keen to capture for the film, invite him to talk about that. Once signed though, you *must* follow through and develop those areas. Woe to the actor with a shabby accent or a weak understanding – your ego will end up on the cutting room floor.

All this is happens in a conversation ranging from 20 minutes to 2 hours, over lunch at a restaurant, or at their production office. For newcomers meeting with unknown indie producers, have your agent or manager in charge of setting the time and place – having a third party with full knowledge of the meeting will help buffer you from creeps and predators.

Other pointers:

- Be on time and reasonably dressed.
- Relax. Tension is the actor's greatest enemy.
- Keep your wit and be a good sport.

And remember, "luck" is very often just preparation meeting opportunity. Break 'em, baby!

THE ABC's OF GETTING AN AGENT

The question I am asked most frequently is, *"How do I get an agent?"*

My Plan A, and the one I consider the strongest approach, is to mail well-thought out, and attractive hardcopy packages that appeal directly to the needs of the agency (whether it be commercial or theatrical). All packages should include a picture, resume, cover letter, and a demo reel (dvd, or link to one in the cover letter).

I devote a great deal of time to this question in my Business of Acting class, and I dedicated an entire chapter (plus additional segments in other chapters) to this very topic in this book. There is so much preparation involved in finding an agent, and all of it must be executed well – from finding the right sized agency, the right person's name and division for submission, to selecting the right headshot, preparing a clean resume, and composing the ever-dreaded cover letter.

Whenever I explain this process, I see the astonishment in the eyes of my actors, and feel their hearts drop. They had no idea it would be so time consuming. But it is. And if you plan ahead, roll up your sleeves, and put in the proper amount of time to do it right, you'll open doors; the right doors.

Many Actors believe an easier path, a Plan B, is to email their materials instead of sending hardcopy. Technically, they're right, it's faster. But, then there's the whole dilemma of an email list – there isn't one. Mind you, there are charlatans out there who, for a mere $300, will give you their "secret" to getting this list. Or you can stop getting scammed, and compile the list yourself. It doesn't cost hundreds of dollars to buy an agency book at Samuel French and Drama Book Shop; or The Call Sheet at Backstage.com; or, join IMDb Pro, and look up each agent individually. These methods are time consuming and will ultimately only net you a lot of "info@ agency" addresses which are already drowning in a tidal wave of submissions. Additionally, agencies will specify whether or not they're even open to emails – most are not – and it will irritate them if you ignore their guidelines. In the event your target agency does not accept email submissions, the odds are high your emails won't even be opened; there are only so many hours in a workday for that weary assistant. Also keep in mind, any direct email to an agent most assuredly falls in their spam folder. An actor can waste weeks waiting for a response that will never come, and time is a precious commodity.

Plan C for some actors is attending an agency showcase. Actors believe they can be discovered and signed through this forum. It happens from time to time but the odds are not in your favor. My opinion is that agency showcases can be a road, but are more useful as a supplemental and secondary effort to the hardcopy packages. For those of you unfamiliar with the agency showcase: all showcases generally require the actor to have a monologue or scene prepared to perform; they're given notes and adjustments afterwards by agents; and the whole session is followed by a Q&A. Agency Showcases should be vetted first to make sure they're legitimate. Go to http://www.dir.ca.gov/dlse/DLSE-Databases.htm and click on "Fee Related Talent Service" for California info.

Actors are often given conflicting advice on how to send out agency queries – knowing who's right and who's wrong can really put your panties in a twist when everyone seems to be an expert on the subject. Here's an anecdote that best describes this dilemma, told to me by a former student who attended an agency showcase: When asked about hardcopy submissions, an agent from a huge agency sneered, "That's so old school. We NEVER take hardcopy, we ONLY look at email submissions." When asked for his email address, he declined. Classic Hollywood runaround. Then again, he was from one of the biggest international agencies out there, so of course he wasn't going to give out his email. Unless you've got a huge resume and are pulling down $250K+ in loose change, they're not interested. Don't waste your time submitting to the biggies, they'll find YOU, not the other way around. The former student who told this story was enrolled in my Business of Acting class, the same class where I'd taken great pains to show how to properly build a hardcopy package. She went for Plan C instead and was so confused by this experience. I don't blame her. I say "do this" and the other guy steps on it. Who do you believe? Well, there's nothing like writing a book on the subject so the universe can test the theories.

I recently went through an agency upheaval and found myself without commercial rep. So, I took my own advice; I thoroughly researched agencies, chose 12-15 that were the right size for my level of experience. I paid close attention to their preferences (found in books and on their websites), then sent hardcopy when requested (about 98%) and email when requested (about 2%). This whole process took about a week and a half to research and another week to assemble. I got immediate responses from the hardcopy, and not a whistle from the emails. Why? Because I took the time to research the right agent; Because I paid attention and read the fine print; Because they're human beings with all five senses – they want to see me, touch the picture, read an intelligent letter written with brevity and wit, then let their God given instincts tell them which way to go. Responding viscerally is immediate and more powerful than the emotional detachment of an email. I submitted to twelve agencies, I was called in to six. In every single meeting, they said they were "so happy to get real materials, so relieved it wasn't an email." I was signed to a new agent in a month.

And that former student? After two years, she still hasn't sent out packages, only 'shortcuts' through showcases and emails because the 'old school' takes too much time.

I'm signed.
She's not.
Get busy.
This works.

REJECTION AND FAILURE AND SURVIVING YOURSELF

One of the most frequent comments I get is "Acting? I could never do that. All that rejection!" The daily dust-off from pounding pavement is discouraging, and I can only pass on the things I eventually learned in order to survive it myself. One of the secrets to tenacity is reverse psychology – I choose to look pragmatically at all facets of the cycle as *opportunities*. And this is a stretch for me, as I'm naturally cynical. These are the things that keep me grounded:

PART 1: ENERGY BREEDS ENERGY

It's a law of physics. The business side of acting is a cycle, and it runs in seasons – Pilot Season, hiatus, Summer Season, hiatus, Episodic Season, winter holidays. You work, you don't work, you work, you don't work. Either I accept the whole picture or I will diminish my energies with unrealistic expectations. My sense of validation has to come from the actions I take to *always* feel like a working actor. In the times I'm not making money, I will take a class, do a reading, learn a new skill (like fencing or a dialect), break down a play, or join an actors' lab. My energy and my acting muscles stay fluid, ready, inspired – and most important, my attitude remains enthusiastic. When I'm blue or shut down because I'm "not working," nothing happens and I'm a real drag. When I'm engaged in something that inspires my interest and enthusiasm, opportunities come.

Sometimes the opportunity is a gig, sometimes the opportunity is developing into the person that the world needs me to be. Opportunity = hope = happiness. I want happiness. I just have to let go of the idea of what that looks like.

PART 2: I'M NOT LUCKY

Fear says "I'm Not Lucky" (i.e. A cursed man is one who thinks he is.) I still believe that luck is not much more than preparation meeting opportunity. Sure, part of luck is something undefinable, random, just out there, unexpected. But how many times have I had the chance to do something cool, yet I lacked the skill and experience to meet the challenge? I can get the audition, but if I can't deliver, then I won't be "lucky." I once showed up for a theatre audition of a Moliere play and, in spite of a lengthy stage resume that implied "ready," I blew large, nasty chunks. Why? I'd never studied Moliere.

Woody Allen said it best: "Ninety percent of luck is just showing up." It's not about showing up for the audition. It's about showing up for myself. I know what my weaknesses are – be it vocally, physically, whatever. If my voice is weak, I show up to voice lessons; if I'm clumsy, I show up to ballet; if I'm frightened, I show up to a scene study or specialty class I've never taken before. I don't have to know where it will lead, I just have to *show up* and turn those defects into assets.

One time I had a long bout with some serious self-esteem issues. So I decided to study Chekhov for several months with a Russian master, and I enrolled in a fencing class. Nine months later, I won a leading role at a Tony Award-winning regional company – the play was set at the turn of the century, the character was a master swordsman. That wasn't an accident, it was preparation meeting opportunity. If I hadn't shown up for those classes, I wouldn't have been "lucky" at the audition. Just work to be better and let the universe open the door.

PART 3: ILLEGITIMIS NON CARBORUNDUM

Illegitimis Non Carborundum is Latin for *"Don't let the bastards get you down."* With every career, life intrudes with heartbreak or corruption. Death, divorce, financial troubles, illness, adultery, drug abuse ... there are so many ways to shake an actor's confidence, and it's so easy to get off course. It's even harder to get back on. I can't count the number of the truly talented people I've seen lose an agent, blow an audition, kill a show, or leave the business because the love of their life had broken their will to go on.

When face with insurmountable heartbreak, here's my set of survival skills:

1. Agree to table the discussion (running obsessively in my head)

2. Leave my bags (of trouble) at the stage door

3. Trust that the universe is watching my back

It's a kind of *modus vivendi*, a temporary ceasefire. Whatever my troubles are, they'll still be waiting for me when I come home. I give myself permission to close the door on them instead of ruining those few creative hours with unnecessary strife.

At one point in my career, I was wonderfully engaged as a leading lady in a Broadway comedy. At the same time, I was drowning in fear, my mind and heart divided about the last toxic stages of a deteriorating marriage. Believe me, I wasn't "feeling" funny and my mind was very busy with my troubles. So every night I made an agreement with myself to "table the conversation" and "leave my bags at the stage door." It was the only way to focus in order to do my job and do it well. Only then was I able to walk clear-minded onto the stage and freely live the part I was hired to play.

Surrender is not defeat. Letting go of despair for two hours allowed the creative spirit to refresh me with courage and delight, and rest my weary heart. I still practice this wisdom. It has never failed me and it has allowed me to not fail myself.

PART 4: LUCK'S NOT MAGIC. IT'S MATH

Play out the odds. Luck's not magic, it's math. Within every gender, age range, and level of talent, there are certain mathematical odds of your winning a part. No one books everything they go for. Let's say you (the talented actor) have the odds that you'll book one out of every 15 auditions. That means you'll have to get through 14 auditions to get to 15. Therefore, every audition cannot be considered a "failure" but just part of the path you must tread in order to reach your goal.

Flip your frame of reference. It is not a "rejection," like you were tossed aside, but a push forward, propelling you on to the next opportunity. Practice gratitude for every milestone met, because that meeting might actually be the trigger for the next gig.

Over time, I learned that I rarely got the first audition. But, if I came in with an open and flexible attitude, if I showed up prepared with interesting choices, the same casting director would remember me down the line and call me back for another role. *You're not there to book the job, you're there to make fans.* Stay focused on your work and let it speak for you. Keep it simple for the audition – just "Suit Up. Show Up. Throw Down. Go Home. "

PART 5: YOU ARE THE COMPETITION

There aren't thousands of actors competing to get ahead. There is only you. You are your competition.

Many years ago I read an interview in a sports magazine on "the fastest man in the world." The journalist said, "You must train very hard to get such speed." The runner replied, "On the contrary, working hard is a total liability. The harder I work, the slower I get. The more I relax, the faster I get." "Interesting," said the journalist, "but what about the man from South Africa? It's said he's behind you by only a tenth of a second." The runner said, "I never look behind me to see who's catching up. In the time it takes me to turn my head, I've shaved a full second off my time."

I then understood more clearly that the best thing I could do for myself was to not worry about the other actress or the producer's lists. Any time spent in fear or speculation would just split my focus and cut into my edge. My edge is my craft and I am obliged to pay attention and breathe. *I am in competition with myself to be better.*

And what about the other kind of competition? The jealousy and back-biting one sometimes encounters on the job? Let's face it, more than once in your career, you'll be booked on a job, and some member of the cast is counting lines, undermining your work, or having a hissy just because you are there. Well. If they're that threatened, then I must be doing something right. It takes a lot of self-control not to bite at the bait and go into battle mode – it affects the whole cast. My teacher, Stella Adler, groomed her actors to think like Leading Ladies and Leading Men. Leading Ladies set the tone. It's my responsibility to set the tone. Take the high road. Take the lead.

You are the competition and you must be doing something right.

PART 6: KNOW THYSELF, DON'T BLOW THYSELF TO BITS

Perfection and the Inner Critic. What actor is ever satisfied with their work? There's always a very fine line between discipline and perfectionism. The minute I'm spiraling downward into self-hatred, I know I've lost my thread on my work.

Self-hatred does not work.
Does not help you.
Does not change you.
Does not serve you.
Period.

Good Dog, Bad Dog. The story goes that there's a good dog on one shoulder and a bad dog on the other. All day long there's a dogfight. The good dog reminds you that you're doing great, she's proud of you, and you should keep up the good work. The bad dog says you're worthless, hopeless, and without talent. All day long there's a dogfight ... who wins? The dog you feed.

Remember that. Feed the good dog ... and strive for excellence, not perfection.

It's important that we discipline our focus to concentrate in such a way that we don't burn out. You must protect the flame. My talent is a small, vital flame that glows in dark, private chambers. Its virtue is the whisper that says "You're beautiful" and "You're doing great" and "Keep up the good work, I believe in you." The creative process is always one of hope. Cling to what is luminous in yourself. Victor Hugo said it best: "Have courage for the great sorrows of life and patience for the small ones; and when you have laboriously accomplished your daily task, go to sleep in peace. God is awake."

PART 7: THE TEN RULES OF SHOW BUSINESS

1. Take the money.
2. Eat when you can.
3. Nothing is in the bag so keep your day job.
4. Never screw the stage manager!!!!
5. Never turn your back on a producer.
6. Leave yourself alone and work to be better.
7. Never share a vast idea with a half vast person.
8. Never forget what they've done to you but never show them you remember.
9. Never underestimate the bad taste of the artistically pretentious.
10. Fame is what others give you: success is what you give yourself.

PART 8: PRAY WITH A FEATHER, NOT A PICKAX

"Pray with a feather, not a pickax," my coach told me after I'd called her in a tiff over some role I was trying to master. "Tension is the actor's worst enemy."

Tiffs and tantrums happen when I'm working too hard in rehearsals or on a set, or when I'm angry or afraid, or if I'm working on a character who is psychologically difficult or beyond my understanding. I used to think I could master that beast if I just put my back into it, and muscled it down to my will.

However, I have learned that the solutions to my creative challenges come more easily if I build breaks into my day after a few hours of intense work. When on a set and my lunch is only a half hour, I power nap with my legs raised above my heart to double the nap time, bringing more oxygen in the blood to my brain ... and I won't wake up groggy in the head.

In rehearsals, I've had countless experiences where I couldn't get inside the character. Defeated and upset, I fell into bed, only to wake up with a marvelous idea or a small effortless insight that resolved the issue. Insight comes when I'm wide open, and that can be achieved only in a tension-free mind and body. Rest.

PART 9: TRAINING?! Isn't There An App For That?

I recently attended a film premiere and a very young, very handsome guy asked if I were an actress. I said, "Yes." He said, "Great! Can I sit next to you?" In the next few minutes, this total stranger gave me a brief but detailed spin of his life: yes, he was an actor, but unemployed. He'd had a series, but it was cancelled. Now his manager wouldn't return his calls, and his recent auditions had been awful and unnerving. I casually suggested that he might use this downtime to take a class, stay fluid for his next break, and feel like a "working actor."

He actually turned pale, stubbornly set his jaw and scoffed, "Training! I wouldn't ruin myself with training!" This beautiful little sun god thought training would smother his natural talent. I sweetly replied that maybe, you know, he could think about it. (After all, if he keeps doing what he's doing, he'll likely keep getting what he's getting – unemployed.)

I understand it, though. I ran on my own "natural instincts" for years. Then I hit a wall. It was like having a race car engine without a license to drive it. Nothing feels worse than knowing I'm a faker, reaching for the same stale bag of tricks. I had to shake that friggin' bag up and learn something new, something larger than just myself. Training didn't kill "me." No. I discovered that it *challenged* me to be a better "me."

Talent on instinct is good, and will get you work, but if you don't grow, you go ...

Training (the right training) gave me *actor muscle.* That has kept me inspired and on-track. It's there to enlarge you, not to entrap you.

I just recently attended several auditions – rooms full of women I've never laid eyes on in my life. I remember I used to see the same pool of women 15 years ago at the rounds. Five years later, some were missing. Another five years, even fewer. Today? One, maybe three. And yet, *I'm still here.* I couldn't help but think about that guy. I hope he thought about me, too, and that took that class.

PART 10: SURVIVING NERVES AND STAGE FRIGHT

Recent question from an actor: *"I'm terribly nervous about an audition next week. Auditioning has always been my weakness. Any pointers?"*

You can't afford to be nervous. Tension is the actor's greatest enemy – it chokes off all creative impulse and heartbeat, rearranges your body and voice into all sorts of tics, kills timing, and we hear the words but do not see a human being having a human experience in truth. Casting doesn't give you an appointment because they want you to suck; on the contrary, they want you to be good. They are rooting for you, so they're not the enemy. No matter how uninspired their "listening faces" are, they are listening; they are not the judge, jury, or executioner.

I've been in the business for 30 years – I still get nervous. I've just learned to absorb it in a way that I don't fall apart. And I have other methods to overcome stress – namely reverse psychology and rehearsal. For me, stage fright has the same symptoms as Christmas morning when I was six years old: my hands sweat, my mind races, my breath is shallow and all my senses are heightened. *The big difference is* the frame of mind. Just flip your reference: stage fright keeps me paralyzed, Christmas morning fills me with anticipation – *I cannot wait to get into the room.*

The other times I'm the most nervous and neurotic are those when I'm not prepared or haven't rehearsed enough – or if I've just rote-memorized words without thought for the experience of the character. Notice I said "experience," not feelings/emotions. Feelings are the first thing to dry up because of adrenalin and nerves. But if I'm rehearsed, if I love that little slice of the character's life and time, and go to the experience of living just that, then the feelings come without force or manipulation. Experience is not just emotions, it's much larger. It's the time of life, the place, the conflict, who you are and who you're talking to, the whole banana. But mostly, experience is *you believing in all of this yourself.* If you don't love your character, you'd better find a way inside of them and make them important. So just love your work, and let the magic happen.

It takes time and experience to build up enough actor muscle (the inner strength) to offset the nerves/stage fright, to stay unflappable ... but you do survive. You learn and you go to the next audition. And the next one is better. And the next one, too. And if you happen to just blow the audition? *So what!* It's not fatal. Take the bullet, tuck and roll, get up, and move on. The most important part of this last bit is to JUST. GET. UP.

PART 11: NEWS AT 11 – SCHMACTOR TAKES HOSTAGES AT CALLBACK

Youngbloods starting in the business, and even some great veteran actors, may think their full rehearsal work is appropriate for an audition, but no, most often not. In auditions, casting and production is gonna give you two minutes to be brilliant. Same with professional theatre. They all have a time limit (anywhere from 2 to 10 minutes total) then it's "Thank you, that'll be all." The artistic life still has to meet the standards of the business world, and time is money.

I know, it's hard to stay alive artistically and stay mindful of the business of acting. My solution? When I have complex characters that demand deep work, I start days in advance of an audition. I work my tail off and I go to treacherous places. I pave the road to hell and I visit it every day. On the morning of the audition, I visit hell again, stay awhile to get my motor hot, then drive to the appointment and *throw down*. Wrestling with all those demons is the kind of stuff that you do privately, in class/lab or rehearsal. With a callback, it's down to just a few actors, so casting and production at this point just want to see it. They don't want to see you working up to it.

Once upon a time, there was a brilliant actor (truly.) He went to a callback for a very difficult play and a superb role, and he was quite perfect for the part. But he spent half an hour onstage in front of them "finding" the character for (at most) a ten-minute scene. He spent the first two minutes confrontationally staring down the director, spitting on the floor, and the next 28 minutes working his paces and breaking up the scene to go inside himself ... and *sometimes* saying the words.

Maybe it was a character choice to shock and offend, but probably not to the effect the actor intended. Two of the producers said they felt like the actor had taken them hostage. The writer was upset that he didn't hear his words. The casting director was cool – loved actors, just said, "Oh, he's really method" – and wasn't that put off (thank God) even though it messed up the appointment times for the rest of the day. As for me, I thought it was ballsy and brilliant, but it cost a most deserving actor a great part, just because he was self-indulgent. If he'd opened with the bold moves, then moved right into the material, he probably would have been cast. I know this guy – he's not insane in performance or life, but the producers don't know him like I do.

I think he actually knew better, but he took the risk anyway. Producers know there are other actors with talent and the self-discipline to show their best in the first few minutes. If you're a star, it's a different discussion. But if you're a worker bee (as most of us are) the producers need to know that you're not going to waste their time, because time is money. Taking 30 minutes to get in sync for a two-page scene is a potential train wreck to a production schedule that has anywhere from 4 to 15 set-ups for each scene. You spend that much time on each take and the producer has some overtime to pay and location contracts to rearrange. Or you'll simply force them to cut your part in post if they can't make time for the proper coverage (medium shots and close-ups) on the front end. In an Equity play, they pay the full company to rehearse, not just you.

The audition setting is where they gauge not only your talent, but whether or not you're ready when they call "Action." Work smart and don't be a baby. There are efficient ways to maintain your artistry, internalize your methods, and streamline your delivery. Prep early, work deep, arrive early, but be ready to throw down when you come in.

They'll think you're a genius if you keep your methods to yourself.

CONCLUSION

Building an acting career is not an exact science. You won't find any hard and fast rules, but there are basic, established methods and protocol. I've shared the ones that I've found the most useful. I cannot promise you a career, but I *can* show you a path toward a career worth having.

Good show.
Break a leg.
Carpe Diem.

ABOUT THE AUTHOR

I'm a Road Warrior, and from Broadway to soundstage I'm still pounding pavement. I studied with the late, great Stella Adler, and am blessed to work in both categories as a Leading Lady and a Character Actress. I do a lot of TV and film these days and have had the good fortune to work under series regular, recurring, and guest star contracts on shows such as "Modern Family," "Rizzoli & Isles," "Criminal Minds," "Mad Men," "Mathnet" and several national and international commercials. I'm also a theatre rat with credits that include Broadway, as Carla/Alaura Kingsley in "City of Angels", Sarah Bernhardt in "Ladies of the Camellias", Miss Hannigan in "Annie", and Trudy in "Club Termina."

I've taught at South Coast Rep, the Stella Adler Academy, and The American Academy of Dramatic Arts. I demand as much skill and clarity in my own work as I do in yours and continue to work my craft weekly with The Actor's Gym, a professional lab for writers and actors.

Find more information at actormuscle.com

Visit IMDb to see my full credits and reel

ACKNOWLEDGMENTS

Amy Bowker, a fantastic writer, for her support and excellent work on proofreading, copy editing, and updating drafts of this book.

Kelly Andersson, who helped me manifest a lifelong dream. I am ever grateful for her incredible editing and design skills, pioneer spirit, and good humor.

Dr. Nina LeNoir, an extraordinary leader and individual. Her dedication, vision, and faith in her students and faculty continue to bless us all.

The industry professionals and organizations who so graciously gave their time and attention to refining the details: Breakdown Services, Casting Networks, Now Casting, Casting Frontier, Backstage, my Union reps at AEA and SAG-AFTRA, my talent agents, A. Chandler Warren, Esq., Mark Lambert with the City Attorney's office, Ian Langtree with Disabled World, David Blank with Redbird Studio and AWOL, and the lovely Scott Steele with URTA.

My friends and colleagues that have weathered my anti-social sequestering and continued to cheer me on, lending their loving friendship toward completing this book: Gloria Hall, Casey Kramer, Karen Hensel, Bobby Moresco, and all the incredible actors and writers with The Actors Gym. Every student (now peers) I have ever had the privilege of teaching has given back in kind, teaching me humility and expanding my own creative heart. Hope and fortitude are gifts I cannot acquire on my own.

There are not enough words to adequately describe the thanks I have for Stella Adler. Her demanding, unerring eye and awe-inspiring teachings have continued to shape and enlarge my life.

Finally, I give thanks to my husband: my best friend, my rock, my Renaissance Man - Christian Meoli.